Information Warfare

For Janet, Beverley and Shona

Information Warfare:
Corporate attack and defence in a digital world

Bill Hutchinson

Mat Warren

 Routledge
Taylor & Francis Group

LONDON AND NEW YORK

First published by Butterworth-Heinemann

First edition 2001

This edition published 2011 by Routledge
2 Park Square, Milton Park, Abingdon, Oxon OX14 4RN
711 Third Avenue, New York, NY 10017, USA

Routledge is an imprint of the Taylor & Francis Group, an informa business

British Library Cataloguing in Publication Data
A catalogue record for this book is available from the Brirish Library

ISBN 0 7506 4944 5

Typeset by Avocet Typeset, Brill, Aylesbury, Bucks

Contents

Computer Weekly Professional Series

Publisher

Mike Cash, Butterworth-Heinemann

Series Editor

Dan Remenyi, MCIL (Management Centre International Limited)

Series Advisory Board

John Riley, Managing Editor, *Computer Weekly*
David Taylor, CERTUS
Terry White, AIS, Johannesburg

There are few professions which require as much continuous updating as that of the IT executive. Not only does the hardware and software scene change relentlessly, but also ideas about the actual management of the IT function are being continuously modified, updated and changed. Thus keeping abreast of what is going on is really a major task.

Computer Weekly Professional Series has been created to assist IT executives keep up-to-date with the management ideas and issues of which they need to be aware.

Aims and objectives

One of the key objectives of the series is to reduce the time it takes for leading edge management ideas to move from academic and consulting environments into the hands of the IT practitioner. Thus, this series employs appropriate technology to speed up the publishing process. Where appropriate some books are supported by CD-ROM or by additional information or templates located on the publisher's web site.

This series provides IT professionals with an opportunity to build up a bookcase of easily accessible but detailed information on the important issues that they need to be aware of to successfully perform their jobs as they move into the new millennium.

Would you like to be part of this series?

Aspiring or already established authors are invited to get in touch with me if they would like to be published in this

series:
Dr Dan Remenyi, Series Editor
(Remenyi@compuserve.com)

Series titles published

IT investment – Making a business case
The effective measurement and management of IT – Costs and benefits (second edition)
Stop IT project failures through risk management
Understanding the Internet
Prince version 2: A practical handbook
Considering computer contracting?
David Taylor's Inside Track
A hacker's guide to project management
Corporate politics for IT managers: how to get streetwise
Subnet design for efficient networks
Information warfare

Forthcoming

Delivering business value from IT
Reinventing the IT department
Delivering IT strategies
e-Business strategies for virtual organizations
How to become a successful IT consultant
How to manage the IT help desk (second edition)
The project manager's toolkit
Network security
E-business
Implementing ERP
IT management

About the authors

Associate Professor Bill Hutchinson is the Associate Head of School of Management Information Systems at Edith Cowan University, Perth, Western Australia. He has 20 years' experience in information systems in government, the oil and finance industries, and academia in Australia and the United Kingdom. His positions have ranged from programmer/analyst, security and database manager, project manager, management information controller, and computer services manager. He is a member of the Australian Computer Society and the Australian Institute for Professional Intelligence Officers, and specialises in information warfare.

Dr Matthew Warren is a senior information systems lecturer in the Department of Computing & Mathematics, Deakin University, Victoria, Australia. He specialises in computer security and information warfare. He is a member of Australian Standards Committee IT/12/4 Security Techniques and is the Australian Representative on IFIP 11 WG 11 – Security Management.

Preface

The idea for this book came out of a need to find a text for a unit in Information Warfare given to Doctor of Business Administration students. Most of the existing texts had a military flavour and so did not suit our task. Others concentrated on security aspects and assumed some level of knowledge in this area. What we wanted was a text that illustrated the uses and abuses of information and its power in the civilian world. Hence, this text was born.

Both authors have a background in information warfare but from different directions. Mat Warren has an interest in security and terrorism, whilst my background is in intelligence systems and management of information and its associated systems. Hopefully, the combination has made for an interesting book.

Another limitation of other texts was the absence of a simple, non-military paradigm for information warfare. Whilst the metaphor 'warfare' will always give the subject a military bias, the revolution in the types of conflict in the contemporary world often makes the purely military context not as useful as it could be.

Civilians are fighting this war and they live in a different world with different paradigms and rules. Therefore, this text is geared for those with a management interest in the topic, although those with a general interest will also find it helpful. It is assumed the main audience will also be working in or around conventional information technology departments. There is a need in this fast, networked world to understand the concepts outlined.

The book itself assumes that readers can apply the principles to their own situation. Examples are given but it is underlying ideas that need to be absorbed. The organisational world is experiencing tremendous change at present. Corporations need to fully understand the importance of their data and the embedded knowledge of their staff to survive. Information warfare theory exposes these needs and points the way to effective organisational change.

The authors welcome comments, and would greatly appreciate any feedback (good or bad!).

Bill Hutchinson

Acknowledgements

Many thanks to Ian Gordon for being patient and allowing the loan of his array of equipment whilst in the UK. To Julie Hawes for meticulously proof reading the text. Thanks to Professor Janice Burn for giving us the time and opportunity to write, and to Dr Dan Remenyi for setting up the publishing.

How to use this book

This text is very much management oriented, rather than technical in nature. Also, it is more concerned with the corporate world than the military. The content is intended to explain the **principles** of information warfare (the abbreviation **I-War** will be used in this book to represent 'information warfare'). Although the text uses examples to reinforce these concepts, it is recognised that rapid changes in technology will make some of the examples rather out of date. Thus concepts are presented (these do not date), and it is hoped that the reader will fill in the gaps by examining their own experience and asking questions about their particular situation. It is meant to enlighten but also to stimulate inventive thinking in this area.

The book is written mainly from an attacker's viewpoint. However, a critical reading should give system defenders some food for thought. The topic raises many contentious ethical issues. This text espouses no philosophy, just ideas about using information as a weapon and also the implication of it being a target. It does not encourage anyone to use these ideas in an illegal or unprincipled way. Morality is the concern of the participants in information warfare, not this book.

It is intended that it be read linearly rather than as separate, individual chapters. The book has two main sections. The first section consists of the initial three chapters and deals with the fundamental principles involved in information warfare. The first chapter should be read before any other (excluding the introduction, of course) as it outlines the models and assumptions used in later chapters. The second chapter examines the organisation of the intelligence function in an organisation and its relationship to information warfare. The third chapter follows on from the first, and examines the specific and important topic of deception.

The next section consists of three chapters concerned with the more specific items relating to threats to computer systems (chapter 4), attack techniques and retaliation (chapter 5), and the more security-oriented defence of systems (chapter 6). Chapter 7 summarises these previous chapters with a proposed risk analysis model. These chapters are more involved with the 'nuts and bolts' of information warfare. This section is completed with a chapter (chapter 8) on the implications of I-War to practising managers.

The next group of chapters deals with some issues associated with I-War: the legal environment of information warfare (chapter 9), the use of the Web by terrorists (chapter 10), and the I-War aspects of the more futuristic use of perceptual intelligence (chapter 11).

The final chapter (chapter 12) speculates on the future of information warfare.

The appendices examine some topics in more detail for those who are interested.

Although the book can be read by those interested in I-War, it can also be used as a course text, and as such has discussion questions that can be used as prompts for seminars, discussion groups, or papers.

The bibliography lists some of the more relevant texts on information warfare. To really become involved in the subject, you should visit Winn Schwartau's web site:

www.infowar.com

This site provides a daily news service, dates for confer-

ences, links to other sites, and access to some pretty
amazing documents. It is free, and a resource that can keep
you up to date with the field. Use it in conjunction with
reading this book. It will bring some of the issues alive.

Bill Hutchinson
w.hutchinson@ecu.edu.au

Mat Warren
mwarren@deakin.edu.au

Introduction

In contemporary times, information technology and its associated systems have flooded the world with data. Information/knowledge components of organisations determine the success of military forces, businesses, states, and individuals. In fact, it is the speed of obtaining, processing, and use of information that has become more important than just having information. It has become one of the fundamental critical success factors for organisational survival. Because of this, it has also grown to be the prime target for combatants in any competitive or antagonistic situation. Information is now not only power but a weapon at all levels: strategic, tactical, and operational. In fact, the Information Age has made these terms become blurred as the speed of data production and the emphasis on the information component of organisations make strategy and operations become the same.

Like all major weapons, information needs to be defended. Therefore, information should be protected as much as physical assets. In fact, it could be argued that it is more important to maintain the integrity and relevance of information and associated systems than it is to maintain physical assets.

This book is an introduction to the concepts associated with the world of information warfare (I-War). It is about a world where organisations use information to build beneficial images of themselves and negative images of competitors or enemies. An environment where hackers attempt to break systems, and deception is the order of the day. It is a world that managers ignore at their peril.

It is a misconception to think that I-War is the sole concern of those running computer systems. Although it is associated with cyberspace, the principles are applicable in any information system. It is the information, and the use to which it is put, that are important. Information technology may be the contemporary vehicle for data and its collection, transmission, processing, and display, but information has always been a factor in competitive situations. The principles are old but the technology is different.

So what is 'information' warfare (I-War)? The term covers the full range of competitive information operations from destroying IT equipment to subtle perception management, and from industrial espionage to marketing. It is about dominating the 'info-sphere'. In military terms, dominating the information battle space has obvious advantages. This is also true for the corporate world. Information superiority is achieved when competitive advantage is obtained from a superior information position. It can be achieved by such things as increasing customers' desire for products, the degrading of competitors' products, the increased effectiveness of operations, superior knowledge of the market, or faster customer response times.

Whilst the aggressive tactics of warfare seem out of place in a corporate world, the principles are very much the same. Of course, blowing up a competitor's computer network is not normal business practice (and is illegal!); the concept of information dominance is not. The aggressive use of information is an option, which should not be ignored by managers surviving in a hostile business world. Although there is much talk of business being 'cooperative' by forming alliances, there are still competitors.

Organisations are not just threatened by conventional business competitors. Others, such as disgruntled employees and pressure groups, can become enemies. Examples such as environmental groups and mining companies have the potential to become combatants in any information war. Think of the potential groups that may be prospective aggressors against your organisations. Organised criminals or terrorists are another source of threat, as are some states that might be using their intelligence agencies to gain business or other confidential information. Even your business partners or clients can become opponents in some circumstances.

In a recent survey carried out by the authors on 111 Australian IT managers, 66% did not think there was any threat of attack from competitors. In fact, 60% did not even have a policy about such things as hacker attacks. This sort of complacency is dangerous, not only in security terms, but also in terms of mindset. If the managers could not imagine competitors using information or its associated technology aggressively, then they are probably not using their own in this way either.

The following chapters will outline the fundamentals of information warfare. These principles are useful to know for both offence and defence. It is primarily concerned with business or government organisations rather than the military perspective, although the martial metaphors do tend to dominate. The book is intended to both interest and enlighten. There are options which are useful to the practising managers, and some which, if carried to excess, can be illegal or unethical. However, knowledge of their existence can only be useful.

I-War is almost the antithesis of security. One is offensive, the other defensive. One tends to be proactive, the other reactive. In any organisation, the two are intimately entwined but require totally different approaches. As the Information Age dawns the ownership, privacy, and speed of access to information will become critical. Managers will need to know that the information they receive has a high degree of integrity, relevance, and timeliness. Competitors wish to keep their own information advantage, and to deprive you of theirs. Some of the methods with which this will be achieved are accepted business practice and some are not. The use and abuse of information will be a critical factor in most organisations' performance in the following decades.

There are three main objectives in I-War:

♦ To use your own information and associated systems to gain advantage over protagonists or competitors.

♦ To protect your own information and associated systems from those who would do them harm by intent or accident.

♦ To formulate strategies and action that produce detrimental effects on your competitors or protagonists.

It is about gaining advantage in the info-sphere. Hopefully, this book will help the reader understand some of the concepts and techniques used. Onward with the battle!

1 | Concepts in information warfare

1.1 Fundamentals

The fundamental weapon and target in I-War is information. It is the commodity which has to be manipulated to the advantage of those trying to influence events. The means of achieving this are manifold. Protagonists can attempt to directly alter data or to deprive competitors of access to it. The technology of information collection, storage, and dissemination can be compromised. Using other, subtler techniques, the way the data is interpreted can be changed by altering the context in which it is viewed.

However, the first thing to be established is the nature of information itself.

1.2 Data, information, and knowledge

The conventional way to define data, information, and knowledge is in a linear fashion. Data describes attributes of things, information is collated data, and knowledge is information which has been interpreted in the light of experience, etc. In the I-War context, a more useful definition can be found in the model proposed by Boisot[1]. In his model, data is associated with a thing, and discriminates between different states of the thing it describes. On the other hand, knowledge is an attribute of an agent (normally, a human being). Knowledge is a set of perceptions about data activated by an event. Information is this set of data filtered by the agent. It establishes a link between the agent and the data. Figure 1.1 illustrates the concept.

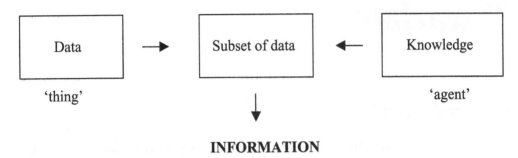

INFORMATION

Figure 1.1: Boisot's model of data, information, and knowledge

The definition of data is fairly simple to understand. Events or items have attributes and descriptions of these attributes are data. However, a human agent decides knowledge. It is established by the history of the person (for example, by education, culture, age, and sex) and the context of the problem at hand. It is this characteristic which makes the idea of 'truth' in information problematic. There might be general agreement about data. For example, everyone might agree that a certain event such as a traffic accident happened. It is not so certain that the witnesses of that accident will agree that the speed of the vehicles was excessive, or that one person is at fault or not. This is more a function of how they saw the accident, where they saw it from, their state of mind, their own prejudices and experiences. (Do they know one of the drivers? Have they recently had an accident? Do they drive fast?) Information is an amalgam of this. Changing the content or timing of the input (data) will change the information derived. Changing the perception of the interpreter will probably be a more long-term proposition. Although it must be said that the television medium does it all the time by manipulating the context of visual images (or by not giving information which puts the images in context). In fact, the combination of edited images (data) and a biased talk-over is a very powerful tool.

Therefore, before the target determines the modes of attack in I-War, the following question should be asked. Is the target the data and/or the human interpreter of that knowledge? Obviously a concerted attack can involve both aspects. In fact, a sophisticated attack will involve both the manipulation of data, and the context within which it is interpreted.

1.3   Basic strategies used in I-War

Using the model developed in section 1.2, the basic tactics can be shown. Figure 1.2 outlines the main attack strategies. From this, it can be determined that if the target is the data, a number of things can be done:

♦ **Deny access to data**: this can be achieved by attacks on hardware or systems containing the data or its collection or deletion of data. As much data has a temporal dimension, it could also involve the delaying of access to data to the point at which it becomes useless.

♦ **Disrupt or destroy data**: this is similar to the above, but disruption can be caused to the system collecting and storing the data, or to that part of the system which disseminates it. Destruction of the data can occur by physical destruction of the storage medium, or the data itself, so it becomes irrecoverable in the time needed to make it useful.

♦ **Steal data**: much corporate data is confidential and can also be of competitive advantage. Theft of this data (and remember, theft of data can go unnoticed as the victim might still have it) might give insights into the workings of the attacked thereby giving the attacker a possible business, negotiation, or criminal advantage.

♦ **Manipulation of data**: data can by added, deleted, or amended to give the attacker advantage. A person committing fraud would often use this method.

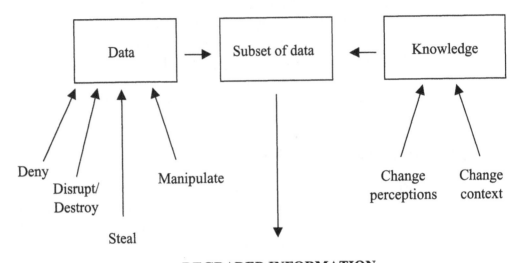

DEGRADED INFORMATION

Figure 1.2: Basic tactics used in information warfare

The strategies to deal with the knowledge (that is, the human) component of information production are basically twofold:

♦ **Change the context in which data is interpreted.**

♦ **Change the perceptions of the people to that data.**

Both of these ideas are closely related. The real difference is that with changing the context, you are trying to alter the situation in which the data is viewed. This can include such things as place, sensory surroundings, and political climate. However, changing perceptions is directed more toward the people themselves, and their thought processes. This can include public relations, advertising, and incentives.

The assumption is that the attacker will **exploit** any situation created by the attack. It is also assumed the victim will attempt some defence. It is the information manager's responsibility to both exploit their own data, and to protect it from others. Other responsibilities should include:

♦ Ensuring the integrity of data collected, both internal and external.

♦ Securing data storage.

♦ Securing the transmission of data.

♦ The effective collation of data for management and operations.

♦ The correct analysis of data to provide knowledge, i.e. the correct reading of the context of the information provided.

♦ The correct dissemination of the knowledge internally, and externally.

The information manager's function is not just the passive one of ensuring the collection and storage of data, as well as ensuring its protection, integrity, and timeliness. It is also to ensure the data is **used** to full advantage. Another function is to examine more aggressive uses of information and systems for their organisation's benefit.

An example of a damaging attack can be seen in exhibit 1.1. This site was hacked after an AirTran crash. One can only speculate on its effect on their demise.

The war over Kosovo in 1999 provided a good example of a type of I-War on the World Wide Web. Both sides had their own web sites, see exhibits 1.2 and 1.3. As well as that, each side had its own hackers, see exhibits 1.4 and 1.5.

It seems that this medium will become a part of future conflicts. The commercial world is not exempt from this process either. See exhibit 1.6 for a successful attack on a fur company.

Exhibit 1.1: The hacked AirTran site

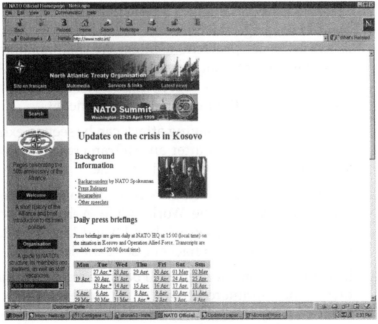

Exhibit 1.2: Official NATO site during the Kosovo conflict

Exhibit 1.3: Web site for Serbian Ministry of Information

Exhibit 1.4: A pro-NATO hack

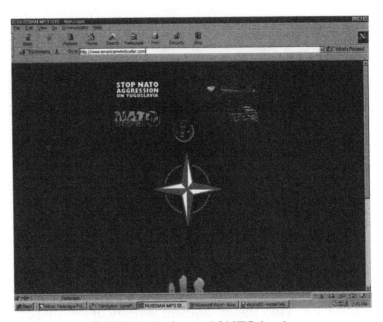

Exhibit 1.5: An anti-NATO hack

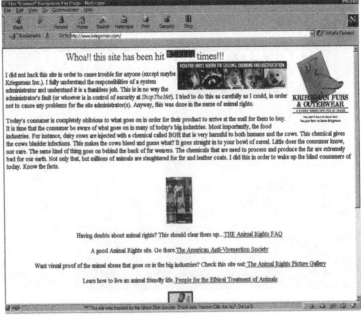

Exhibit 1.6: Successful attack on a fur company site

1.4 A framework for an information attack

The potential elements in an information system, which are prone to attack, are[2]:

♦ **Containers**: for example, computer and human memories.

♦ **Transporters**: for example, humans, telecommunication systems.

♦ **Sensors**: for example, scanners, cameras, microphones, human senses.

♦ **Recorders**: for example, disk writers, printers, human processes.

♦ **Processors**: for example, microprocessors, humans, software.

From these elements, and the model presented in section 1.2, it is possible to develop a simple, generic model of an automated information system. This is presented in figure 1.3.

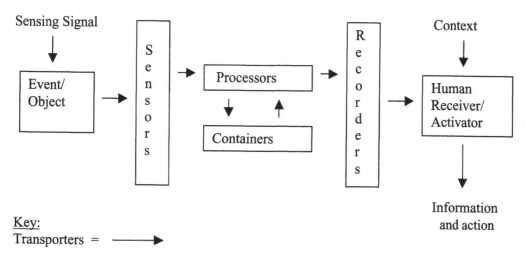

Figure 1.3: Components of an information system

Each one of the elements, and the means by which they can be attacked, are briefly explained below.

Sensors

Here the objective of an attacker is either to destroy the sensor (for example, an electromagnetic pulse with electronic equipment), or 'blind' it to incoming signals (by nullifying or distorting the signal), or to feed it signals that you want it to sense. For example, if submarines can be tracked by satellite monitors from the bioluminescence created by their propellers, then creating similar bioluminescence where there are no submarines will 'fool' the sensor.

Sensors may be active or passive. For instance, a sonar system sends out a signal. The reply is then 'sensed'. However, many sensors are passive and receive signals from an object or event without initiating a sensing signal. In the case of active sensors, the objective is to disrupt this signal. For instance, the 'Stealth Bomber' scatters radar signals which would normally illuminate an aircraft. Another ploy is to create false signals which nullify the sensing signals.

Event/object

This is the item to be sensed. This could range from a building under satellite surveillance to a keystroke on a keyboard. Objects can be camouflaged, and events distorted. So the building under surveillance can be made to look like a housing estate when it is really a factory, or the keystroke represents an 'A' when really the 'B' key has been pressed. The needs here are to assess 'what' is sensed, and 'how' it is recognised. It is a case of showing the sensor what you want it to see, not what is actually there, or what has actually happened.

An attacker will attempt to fool the sensor that the object is not what it really is by such activities as camouflage or other means of hiding. Events need to be made either undetectable or appear to be something which they are not (for example, the publishing of false market indicators).

Processors

Here the main objective of an attacker is to destroy/disrupt the processor, or to alter the logic of the process to achieve the output desired. In computer systems this latter effect can be achieved by alteration of program logic (for example, by a 'virus'), or parameters fed to those programs.

Containers

These data stores can be corrupted by amending, deleting, or adding to them a beneficial way to the attacker. Hacking into databases to change their contents is an example of this.

Recorders

Very much like the sensors, the objective is to destroy/disrupt the recorder, or to corrupt the output (rather than input) stream formation. The manipulation of the workings of these mechanisms (or their logic if separate from main process logic) in a meaningful way to the attacker can be used to provide benefits.

Context

All data is interpreted in a certain context. The objective of the attacker in this element of the chain is to manage perception. Military style psychological operations or commercial style advertising can achieve this. The aim is to produce an environment in which the human will interpret the data in a specific way.

Human receiver/activator

The data produced by the system, and the context it is perceived to be in, results in information creation and action. In a completely automated artificial intelligence system, corruption of the rules upon which decisions are made could cause deception to occur. In human subjects, direct mind manipulation can also achieve this. Such things as behaviour modification (for example, reinforcement, conditioning, punishment), hypnotism, brain washing, or psycho-drugs can cause a deceptive process to occur. Other intimidating techniques such as 'cyberstalking' (that is, the use of email, or other electronic devices to stalk a person) can be used to alter the behaviour of target persons.

Designing an information attack strategy should start off with the proposed, desired effect. The tactics used can then be gleaned from the framework, based on the most effective outcome, and the most vulnerable element of the system in that situation[3].

The previous parts of this chapter have dealt with attack postures. Of course, the victim should not be passive in this process. In this defensive mode, the concept of a 'surprise attack' becomes useful. Whilst security measures may be in place, the world is dynamic and sources of attack unpredictable. It is up to the manager not to be caught unawares.

1.5 The surprise attack

Obviously, any successful but preventable attack is a surprise. Although the previous part of this chapter developed attack strategies, there must also be a defence effort made.

Thus the idea of stopping a surprise attack must be made. However, many I-War attacks are not detected, that is what makes them successful. Therefore much of the defence strategy must be an attempt to predict possible scenarios, rather than just defend against known risks. Pro-activity not just reactivity must be the order of the day.

There is a continuum of 'surprise'[4], from a predictable attack, for which one is prepared (for example, computer viruses), to a strike, which has never been envisaged, and so there have been no preparations at all. An information manager must attempt to envisage what kind of attack could occur as well as when, where and how. This implies not only knowledge of the technical aspects of the systems being managed, but also the people (competitors, staff, clients, criminals, etc.) who are likely to have an impact on the system.

A surprise attack is a function of the victim's expectations and assumptions. It can be caused by complacency. For example, complete reliance on firewalls to protect computer systems, rather than coupling this with continuous monitoring of the internal technical and staff environments, as well as the external world. A system of reaction and prediction must be in place to dynamically cope with the ever-changing environment.

Many managers have an 'it will not happen to me' syndrome. This feeling of invulnerability, optimism, and non-perception of risk is perfectly understandable. It is often the manager who has installed the security and monitoring system. Hence, it has been installed within the constraints of the corporate and individual mindsets. It probably could be achieved in no other way. The problem arises when it becomes fixed in behavioural concrete. I-War is fast moving in terms of technical possibilities. Standing still really means going backwards in this situation.

In the conventional world of intelligence, the capabilities and intentions of potential adversaries are established to develop protective measures. With this in mind, indicators and warnings are monitored to ascertain what the potential adversary is actually doing. In an environment where the number of potential adversaries is limited, and there is time to establish values for any indicators and warnings monitored, then this situation can be effective. However, in the rapid, contemporary world of the Internet where the number of potential attackers is almost infinite, and time is at a premium, this mode of operation is not enough. What is needed is **speed**. The emphasis must be on rapid detection and equally rapid response. This time-based approach has probably always been appropriate, but in the frenetic atmosphere of automated network service denials and speed of light electronic commerce, it is essential.

1.6 The networked society

In the last few years, the concept of the 'virtual organisation' has developed. This organisation is a part of an interconnected network. Each element is a part of a web. The concept is appropriate to describe the internal functions of some organisations, as well as the relationships it has with other entities. This idea can be taken further to whole societies. A useful model[5] explains social development in terms of increasing complexity. Each society is at a different stage of development. However, each society at a higher development level still has elements of the 'lower' stages embedded in it.

The posited stages are:

♦ **Clans/tribes**: primitive, based on family/culture, for example Indian villages, modern street gangs. Communications are based on symbols.

♦ **Institutional**: agricultural, based on state/government, for example, Cuba? Communications are based on writing and printing.

♦ **Market**: industrial, based on economics, for example, Chile? Communications are based on telephone and telegraph.

♦ **Organisational networks**: post-industrial, for example, USA. Communications are based on digital networks.

In terms of information warfare, each society has its advantages and vulnerability. For instance, the USA has an enormous advantage in digital facilities from fibre optic communications to satellites and sophisticated software production. However, this advantage also adds vulnerability, as digital systems are susceptible to attack. However, true networks do have the advantage of being resilient. For example, if one node on the Internet is attacked another can take its place, thereby localising the damage. However, the infrastructure of a 'networked' society (for example, power, water) is exposed, as they are not often true networks. Companies with advanced network capabilities also have the same advantages and disadvantages as those of networked states.

Developing countries at a lower level of development have an advantage of slower communication and processing systems, but this lack of sophistication lessens the vulnerability to an information attack.

The advantages of developed (networked) societies can be summarised as:

♦ Advanced infrastructure.

♦ Have the intellectual property rights to most advanced developments.

♦ Advanced technologies.

♦ Have control of large corporations.

♦ Advanced networked society possible, reliant on technology but infinitely flexible.

♦ Capable of information dominance strategies.

♦ Dominate perception management industries, for example the media.

The advantages of developing nations can be summarised as:

♦ Lack of vulnerable electronic infrastructure.

♦ Low entry costs to get into electronic systems development.

♦ Web-based systems know no geographic boundaries (in theory); hence neither does the 'place' of a company.

♦ Networked societies based on 'clans' are difficult to penetrate.

♦ Cheap labour, often with an educated elite, for example India.

Strategies and tactics used in I-War need to be tailored to the social situation. In a nation-to-nation conflict, this is obvious. However, at a corporate level, the same model of development can be laid over to classify the level of the target organisation. The approach when attacking a street gang should not be the same as that used against a large multinational.

Thinking of organisations as elements in networks changes the approach to competition. The organisation is immersed in the communications environment of all the others. Here data tends to be common. Security of data tends to be superfluous. This, of course, is not true about purely operational and confidential data such as personnel medical records, but rather the environmental data needed to make management decisions. In this environment, it is not so much the availability of data that matters but rather the speed of access and processing of it.

It is important when developing I-War strategies to conceptualise your organisation and any target organisation both as entities in themselves, **and** elements within a network of other organisations and elements. Figure 1.4 shows diagrammatically the change from an individual hierarchy to seeing that organisation either as a network or a part of a network.

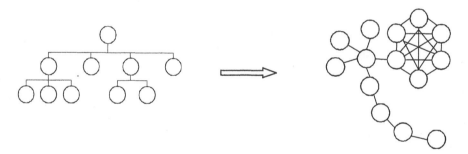

Figure 1.4: An organisation as a hierarchy and as a network

1.7 Some specific techniques in I-War

To sum this chapter up; there are a number of ways information or information systems can be used to gain advantage over (or disadvantage to) another organisation. Examples of some aggressive tactics are:

♦ Information can be manipulated or 'created' (disinformation) to provide the target or its environment (for example, clients) with a perception that develops behaviours detrimental to the target, or beneficial to the attacker. At one level, this can be viewed as advertising, and at another, deliberate deception.

♦ Information can be intercepted thus giving the interceptor an advantageous insight into the target's strengths, weaknesses, and intentions. This information can be gained legitimately, or illegitimately.

♦ Information flows in the target organisation can be disrupted, or stopped, thereby interfering with the normal processes of the target producing an advantage for the attacker.

♦ A target organisation can be 'flooded' with information, thereby slowing or stopping effective processing or analysis of the incoming information.

♦ Information can be made unavailable to a target organisation by destroying the storage medium, or cutting off the information source.

♦ Disrupting the availability of data, or making the system produce incorrect/dubious output, can lower the credibility of information systems.

♦ Confidential or sensitive information can be exposed to the public, clients, government agencies, and so on, thereby embarrassing or in other ways harming the organisation.

♦ Physical attacks on IT or other components of the system can be made.

♦ Subversion of the people who operate the systems can be attempted.

♦ Physical destruction of information (erasure or overwrite) without harming the infrastructure components can be effected.

♦ Logic attacks (malicious code) on system components can be executed.

Obviously, many of these tactics are not pertinent to the contemporary business world (at least, not any ethically based corporate strategy) but they do give an idea of the range of possibilities open to an attacker.

The form of attack can be varied. It depends on such factors as the medium of information transfer and storage (for example, electronic, telephone, verbal, facsimile, etc.), the legality of the attack, and the technology used (for example, electronic surveillance, computer viruses, and human senses).

Notes

1 Further details of his ideas can be found in Boisot, M.H. (1998) *Knowledge Assets*, Oxford University Press, Oxford.

2 These definitions were derived from Denning, D.E. (1999) *Information Warfare and Security*, Addison Wesley, Reading, Mass.

3 See Appendix 1 for a table (A.1), which can be used to plan an attack strategy using this model.

4 Many of the ideas for this section come from Kam, E. (1988) *Surprise Attack*, Harvard University Press, Cambridge, Mass.

5 This model was developed by Arquilla and Rondfeldt, and can be found in Arquilla, J., Ronfeldt, D. (1996) *The Advent of Netwar*, Rand Corporation, Santa Monica.

2 Information as an intelligence weapon

2.1 The intelligence function

It is necessary for any organisation to develop and uphold security standards and precautions which address the potential for attack. There must be frequent reassessment of risk factors. Whilst the overemphasis on potential dangers can create security procedures which stifle organisational development, each risk should be assessed and, at least, some contingencies created to deal with it. Warnings of potential attack should not be ignored (a common phenomenon – 'it has happened to others but not to me'). Innovations by potential adversaries should be recognised. All of this requires an efficient and effective corporate intelligence function. It is this factor that will be examined in this chapter.

Any adaptive and viable organisation[1] needs to possess five main functional areas:

♦ Policymaking.

♦ Intelligence and planning.

♦ Control (and audit).

♦ Co-ordination.

♦ Operations.

The operational, co-ordinating, and controlling functions are there to ensure the efficient and effective running of the system. Information regarding the operational performance of the system is synthesised and fed into the controlling function, which then sends it to the intelligence and planning function. This is all internal information. The intelligence and planning function takes this and information from the external environment, analyses it, and offers the policymaking function some alternative scenarios. The policymaking function then makes decisions, and passes them through the intelligence and planning function to be interpreted and presented to the controlling function to enforce the policies on the operational units. Information flow from the intelligence and planning function into the environment is important to most organisations as a means of manipulating its environment. It does this by feeding its environment information (for example, the market, clients, government agencies) that creates an image conducive to its own organisational interests. In modern parlance, it produces its own 'spin'.

Figure 2.1 summarises the data flow into and from the intelligence function. The authors interpret the intelligence function as that which analyses information to make decisions and hence real world changes. It is a fundamental management function. It is also responsible for any counter-intelligence operations. That is, it must ensure that any protagonists are not able to use methods to the detriment of your organisation.

It is another assumption of the authors that the information/knowledge management function in an organisation is responsible for all information whether internal or external in nature, and if it is flowing around the organisation internally, or to or from the external environment. It does not assume that this is all done by a single entity within the system. When viewed from this perspective the opportunities for manipulation of data and its misinterpretation are manifold. The information/knowledge manager has to ensure the integrity of internal systems, data flowing from

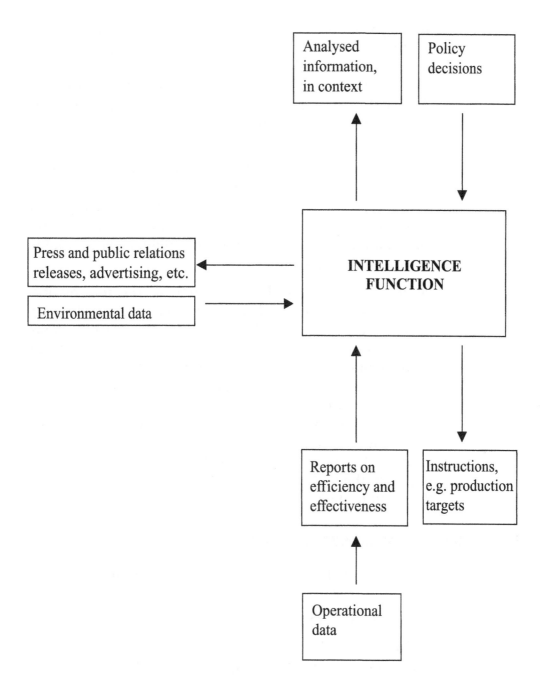

Figure 2.1: Informative flow and the intelligence function in an organisation

the organisation, and that flowing into the organisation. If this, all encompassing, nature is accepted, there appears to be a need to integrate such functions as security, public relations, advertising, and information systems. This will ensure a system which co-ordinates, secures, distributes, and uses information, in whatever form, effectively.

It is important to realise that data comes in many forms and across many media. It can be quantitative and/or qualitative, accurate or speculative, observation or gossip. It is important that management realise that all data can be important, not just data output from the formal computer or paper-based systems.

Figure 2.1 illustrates the magnitude of the information manager's problem, and the numerous avenues that an attacker has. This figure describes the raw, internal, operational data (internal data) being used in collated form to produce management reports (internal 'information'). This information is fed into the intelligence function, as is environmental scanning data (external data) to provide the raw material to be analysed providing intelligence (the intelligence product not the function). This intelligence is provided to the policymaking function, and policies are fed back into the system. Using these policies, instructions are then sent to the operational functions for action.

2.2 Offensive and defensive operations

There are really two fundamental aspects of the intelligence function:

♦ **Intelligence**: the exploitation of information.

♦ **Counter-intelligence**: the protection of the corporate information and knowledge bases, and the disruption of those of competitors.

Both of these can involve offensive and defensive measures[2]. However, intelligence involves the more defensive measures such as the collection, analysis, and interpretation of data, threat analysis, and perception management (for example, public relations and press releases). Counter-intelligence tends to deal with the surveillance and penetration of potential protagonists.

Defensive operations are concerned with protective measures, such as:

♦ The availability and integrity of data.

♦ The confidentiality of data and information.

♦ Recovery of data.

♦ Verification of messages.

When dealing with computer systems, defensive operations comprise such things as:

♦ Encryption policies

♦ Virus checkers

♦ Firewalls

♦ Digital signatures

♦ Access control

♦ Physical and hardware security.

On the other hand, offensive operations are concerned with two basic functions:

♦ To capture data/information from various sources.

♦ To obtain the data/knowledge of others for the benefit of the organisation.

Offensive operations on computer systems involve such things as:

♦ Implanting of malicious code.

♦ Network denial attacks.

♦ Hacking to obtain or manipulate data.

Offensive operations can also involve such things as the spreading of biased information or straight misinformation. The latter techniques bring ethics and legality to the foreground. However, they are being used on a daily basis, so awareness of them is essential for any senior information professional.

2.3   The intelligence cycle?

The classic *modus operandi* of the intelligence function can be found in the intelligence cycle, which comprises:

♦ Setting the target for investigation.

♦ Collection and validation of data.

♦ Processing of data.

♦ Analysis and production of information.

♦ Appropriate and timely dissemination of information.

This approach is appropriate for all intelligence operations, but with some provisos. In the speedy, contemporary climate, the process to produce intelligence must be equally fast. Also, as the area of interest to management may change like the wind and be totally unpredictable except in the short term, the idea of 'setting the target' (or 'setting the boundary of the investigation') may be redundant. This activity may have to be done in 'real time'. The intelligence cycle is more obviously suited to specified medium- to long-term projects rather than general, environmental scanning, which really does not know the boundaries of potential elements of interest until they happen.

Having said that, it would not seem credible to make informed management decisions without collecting data, verifying its source and integrity, processing and analysing as well as, distributing it to those who need to be included in the decision-making process. The electronic world moves at a hasty pace, and so many of these decisions are taken from humans and given to machines. Hence, much data interpreted at a human pace becomes redundant. Recent behaviours of computer driven, stock buying systems have shown that. Does this mean the intelligence function as it has been known in the past is no longer valid? Can computer-based decision-making systems replace human involvement? If it is the case, the vulnerability of them to sophisticated, electronic attack will increase, as will the likelihood of its success.

So what should the intelligence function do? There are four main areas of activity with which it needs to be effective:

♦ Environmental/internal scanning.

♦ Information production for the external world.

♦ Countering detrimental information.

♦ Security of data.

The security function will be examined in later chapters, whilst the others are looked at below.

2.4 Environmental/internal scanning

It is fairly self-evident that an organisation needs to know the happenings of its internal operations and the environment in which it exists, before it can make rational and effective decisions about how it is to proceed. Whilst internal information systems of most organisations are well advanced, those concerned with external data are often not. Internally, the data required is available and can be formatted in a way favourable to integrated databases and such like. The use of data warehouses and data mining enhances the potential of internal data by finding patterns that are not obvious. In a way, they create knowledge. However, it must be said that, despite incredible benefits, there are often situations where there are self-imposed limitations to these. The first is that although the data may be there, it may not be used; so when flags are initiated they are not acted upon. The other limitation on internal systems is that much formal and easily formatted data, such as client details, production figures, and income, is stored but there are no useful systems collecting data on the hazier topics such as staff morale. This can lead to management using the quantitative data to formulate policy to the exclusion of the more intuitive-based material. Whilst the security blanket of figures gives managers a justification for their actions, it does not mean the best decisions are made.

To make good decisions the state of the organisation and its potential must be known. However, it must be known in the context of the dynamic environment it lives in. The scanning of the environment is an ongoing management process. It is the responsibility of the intelligence/information management function to provide this data to decision makers. Marketing departments often have the skills necessary for this. Although they tend to be narrow in their data collection area, their brief can be expanded to cover other areas of intelligence gathering.

The external world is a much messier place in terms of data collection than the internal one. Data comes in many formats and through many media. The areas of interest change, although many can be ongoing. Table 2.1 provides some idea of the potential areas of interest for an organisation over a period of time.

Table 2.1: Some environmental elements of interest and their possible sources

Area of interest	Possible source
Market trends	Media, service providers
Political situation	Media, contacts, politicians, political commentators
Technological advances	Industry press, internet, conferences, industry shows, industrial espionage
State of competitors	Media, annual reports, internet, sales force, informal meetings with competitor's staff at conferences, social and industry events, industrial espionage
Pressure groups	Media, press releases, internet sites, informers, law enforcement, politicians
Terrorist/criminal activity	Media, internet sites, law enforcement, informers
Industrial relations	Media, staff, corporate lawyers, court system
Legal trends	Media, industry press, lawyers, politicians/local authorities
Industry trends	Media, industry press, industrial espionage, contacts in competitors employment, staff

Table 2.1 is certainly not exhaustive and every organisation will have its own set of items it needs to be kept informed of. Sources can vary from those openly available to the public, those that are available commercially, or those that are internally driven. Some imagination must be used to derive sources of relevant data. For example, banks who finance large land purchases could use openly available

satellite imagery to inspect such things as the level of pollution, or soil erosion in the proposed purchase. Also, the data would be useful for inspecting the surrounding land and its influence on the land's potential. For instance, is it in a flood plain?

Open sources include the Internet (a mass of 'information' but it must be used with care as, to put it mildly, it contains some biased content), the press, television, and so on. Professional information providers also produce specialised services commercially. Internally driven data collection may involve the hiring of external, or the use of internal, staff to examine sources of threat or competition. In fact, internal staff can be the source of much intelligence and their potential as a source of knowledge and intelligence is often undervalued.

The knowledge base of most organisations is a vast, and mostly untapped, resource. Staff should be encouraged to divulge any knowledge of interest. Here is the rub. This knowledge is useless if it does not reach those involved in decision making in a timely manner. An incentive scheme must be implemented so staff can actually transmit this knowledge. Hierarchies and self-interest often prevent this. In fact, there is often an active disincentive to disclose. Data can be obtained by the sales force on the road, meetings at industry fairs, casual social meetings, or any of a myriad of sources. An efficient internal data collection system is one which transmits important business intelligence as fast as it does news of office affairs. These systems can be formal or informal, but they must ensure that they treat staff as a network rather than a hierarchy, and they must be trusted. If people see there is some point in them, they will work.

Collection methods can also vary. They may be overt or covert depending on the source or the sensitivity of the data.

2.5   Information production for the external world

An organisation needs not only to collect data to better make decisions; it also needs to use information to project itself to the world. It is important to provide the information needed for clients, government agencies, the public, suppliers, pressure groups, the media, and so on. This information should be presented in a way that gives a good 'spin' for the organisation. It should be used for the betterment of organisational goals.

Any messages sent from an organisation to the outside world should address such items as perception, message encoding, and the nature of the message's language. In other words, it is not just the raw data that needs to have integrity; it is the implied meaning of the message as well. Changing, deleting, or altering words, pictures, sounds, or other stimuli can manipulate this meaning. In the next chapter, the concept of deception will be explored. This can be used both for and against an organisation.

Contemporary organisations use advertising to promote their products and services in a proactive way, and public relations to protect their image (often in a reactive way). These functions must both be ongoing and proactive. It is better to build a context for any situation than to have one foisted upon you. Control of perceptions about an organisation is important for both outside dealing and internal stability. Information about an organisation should not be treated as a free good, but a valuable asset. In fact, an asset that gives competitive advantage. One which is given away when, and only when, it is beneficial for the organisation to do so.

This implies that the data, knowledge, and information within the organisation are known, and given a value. The value of data can be established by a combination of the following factors:

- Cost of obtaining it.

- Cost of replacement.

- Its uniqueness and the business advantage this gives.

- The cost to sales and future development if divulged to a competitor.

- The damage/benefit it could cause if divulged to the public, authorities, clients, suppliers, pressure groups, etc.

- Its sensitivity.

- Legal and ethical need to keep private.

- Legislative need to keep.

- Operational need.

- Potential for future business use.

These factors must be used when determining the level of information security. They must also be used when determining its use in the public and business arena. The value of data, information, and knowledge should be made clear to staff, and controls put in place to ensure that really important information is only divulged when it should be. This can be extremely difficult as apparently innocuous data can give important information given the context. For instance, a casual remark about a future sales trip to town X might indicate to a competitor that you are moving in on a client. A request for redundancy payout figures might flag a downsizing is about to occur. In fact, the authors know of a case of a bank manager who was contacted by an over-zealous insurance agent trying to get the manager to invest his severance payout in a financial product. However, the manager was not officially told of his impending dismissal for another two days.

2.6   Countering detrimental information

In the case where information has leaked or a third party has released information or disinformation detrimental to the organisation, then a reactive process must occur. This is really the same process as that outlined in the previous section. Only now a third party has set the context.

A campaign of action must be formulated, and the following actions taken:

♦ Determine the source of the information and take action to avoid a recurrence.

♦ Determine the damage done to corporate image, sales, etc.

♦ Determine any legal actions that can be taken.

♦ Determine the end result wanted by management of any action.

♦ Determine if it is best left alone; if not, continue.

♦ Determine the message to be sent and the target for that message. The target may be an audience or a 'victim'.

♦ Determine the most appropriate medium for that message, both in terms of presentation and communication.

♦ Determine any legal ramifications of your counteraction.

♦ Determine cost and benefit of action.

♦ Determine any possible consequential implications of action.

♦ Execute plan of action.

♦ Monitor for any detrimental consequences of action.

The use of deception will be examined in the next chapter,

but the fundamental principle is that information is a construct from data (both true and false) and knowledge (both rational and irrational). This information should be used and constructed for the benefit of the organisation and its staff, shareholders, and other stakeholders. It is the task of the intelligence function to do that.

2.7 An intelligence department?

The intelligence function is obviously important to an organisation, but does it necessarily follow on that a special department needs to be created? The answer lies in the type of industry and its environment, and how the existing functions, comprising the roles of intelligence, operate.

Any separate intelligence department would have to be under control of, and have direct access to, senior management. It would have to formulate data gathering strategies at the strategic, tactical, and operational levels. It would have to plan and execute data gathering activities. Also, the counter-intelligence function may come under its wing. Of course, this not only includes security but more active operations to minimise any threats to the organisation. Its access to highly important and sensitive data and knowledge necessarily means that its staff must be chosen carefully.

A department with these functions would indeed be a powerful one. Its right to access internal and external material might make it a risk to the organisation. Therefore, strong controls and limitations on it need to be in place. The pervasiveness of information technology in the intelligence and other organisational processes would intuitively point to the function being a part of information services. Again, this depends on the nature of the existing department in this area. The providers of information systems (IS) tend to be technically oriented. Their roles are seen to be delivering and protecting the data rather than utilising it advantageously in an aggressive way. Although some IS departments do give advice on the use of technology, or how to present information and such like, few give real business advice on how to use information. The advent of data mining might allow some IS personnel to transfer to the intelligence function, at least on the data gathering side. However, it is the targeting and analysis of data that is the core of intelligence.

Staff in the intelligence department must have the ability to look at situations from various perspectives, for example that of competitors, clients, criminals, and so on. It is this skill which enables a complete threat analysis to be attained. Looking at the problem solely from the corporate or individual manager's viewpoint will lead to misjudgements. The likelihood and consequences of threats must be evaluated. Potential attackers must be appraised in terms of not only their capabilities but also their likely intentions. These are not roles for the untrained amateur.

In a sense, intelligence gathering is certainly the responsibility of all managers, and to a certain extent, all staff. Therefore, any intelligence department needs to ensure that efficacious systems are in place to facilitate this. The all-encompassing nature of this function can produce a stifling effect as, also can too much emphasis on security. Risk must be balanced against flexibility and development. No system is perfect, so some level of error must be accepted. This is the stuff of management – decision making. This always requires some risk (if there is no risk, there is no decision to be made). In the modern, knowledge-based world, it is the proper use of intelligence that can give an organisation the competitive edge.

Chapters 1 and 2 have concerned themselves with the general principles involved in I-War. The following chapters deal with the specifics involved. Chapter 3 deals with techniques used for deception, whilst the following three chapters deal with the specifics of computer-based I-War. They encompass threats to computer systems, attack strategies using computer systems, retaliation against computer-based attacks, and defence from them.

Notes

1 The Viable System Model was developed by Stafford Beer. For more information see: Beer, S. (1984) The Viable System Model: its provenance, development, methodology and pathology. In, Espejo, R., Harnden, R. (eds), *The Viable System Model*, John Wiley & Sons, Chichester, pp. 211–270, and Beer, S. (1985) *Diagnosing the System for Organisations*, Wiley, Chichester.
2 Some of the concepts presented in this section were derived from Waltz, E. (1998) *Information Warfare: Principles and Operations*, Artech House, Boston.

3 | Deception

3.1 Principles

The uses of deception in natural systems and organisations are manifest. The natural world contains innumerable examples of camouflage and behaviours, whose purpose is to confuse or to create illusion. Examples include the octopus that changes colour to match the ocean bottom, or the bird that feigns injury to distract a predator away from its young. In organisations, there is a myriad of behaviours that are intended to create an illusion, from ubiquitous advertising to the well-formatted and favourable annual report. In fact, deception is a fundamental aspect of strategy.

Basically strategic plays can be divided into two types[1]: those for the powerful and those for the weak. Although it is an overgeneralisation, the strong can use 'force' as their strategy, whilst the weak must rely mostly on deception to gain an advantage[1]. Of course, the strong can use deception as well, but there are fewer requirements for them to do so.

In this book, the word 'deception' is used to denote **an action, which changes data, objects, or context for the benefit of the agency changing them**. Although the word itself tends to have a negative connotation, deception is neither 'good' nor 'bad'. Perhaps the ethical implications of deception can be found in the motives for its use. In I-War based in the corporate world, the use of deception is the major strategy.

Table 3.1 summarises the act of deception. If a message is manipulated and the receiver accepts the message, then deception has occurred. Also, if the message has not been modified, and the receiver rejects it because of the active manipulation of the context in which the message has been interpreted, then deception has again occurred.

Table 3.1: Message acceptance and deception[2]

	Message untouched	Message manipulated
Message accepted	X	**Deceit has occurred**
Message rejected	**Deceit has occurred**	X

Deception is basically about changing information. The model developed in chapter 1 and shown in figures 1.1 and 1.2 can be modified to include only deception and is presented in figure 3.1. Hence, if someone wishes to influence or attack an entity via the information derived by it, then **data** can be deleted, changed, or added; similarly the **context** that data is examined can be influenced (so influencing the interpretation of that data).

Heuer[3] states:

People construct their own version of 'reality' on the basis of information provided by the senses, but this sensory input is mediated by complex mental processes that determine which information is attended to, how it is organized, and the meaning attributed to it. What people perceive, how readily they perceive it, and how they process this information after receiving it are all strongly influenced by past experience, education, cultural value, role requirements, and organization norms, as well as the specifics of the information received.

Hence, people view the world through a constructed reality. Thus, deception is achieved by altering the mental models of the target, and/or the data fed to the mental processes.

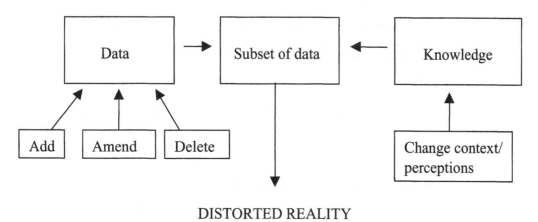

DISTORTED REALITY

Figure 3.1: Tactics to deceive

Deception is an integral part of I-War. Corrupting data and changing attitudes to produce a desired state of mind is one of the most powerful aspects of I-War. For instance, if a web site has obviously been attacked it might make for embarrassment, but the subtle changing of attitudes against or for an item by undetected changes is much more effective in the long term.

3.2 Types of deception

Deception[4] can be classified into two main types:

♦ Level 1: Hiding the real.

♦ Level 2: Showing the false (although this always involves some form of 'hiding' as well).

These fundamental types are further divided into six categories of deception

<u>Hiding</u>

♦ **Masking**: blending in, for example camouflage.

♦ **Repackaging**: something is given a new 'wrapping'.

♦ **Dazzling**: confounding the target, for example codes.

<u>Showing</u>

♦ **Mimicking**: a replica, which has one or more character-istics of reality.

♦ **Inventing**: creating a new reality.

♦ **Decoying**: misdirecting the attacker.

Table 3.2 gives some examples of different types of deception in the natural and human worlds, whilst table 3.3 gives some examples found in computer/network systems.

Table 3.2: Examples of types of deception

Type of deception	Examples
Masking	Camouflage found in some animals, which blends them with natural surroundings. For example, the colour changes in some squids or the chameleon.
Repackaging	Cosmetics/make-up, padded clothing, etc.
Dazzling	Ink squirted from an octopus to confuse predators, or chaff discarded by Second World War bombers to confuse radar.
Mimicking	Bird feigning injury to distract predator from young.
Inventing	Propaganda, public relations, advertising.
Decoying	Replica tanks used in Kosova war by Serbs.

Table 3.3: Examples of types of deception in computer/network systems

Type of deception	Examples
Masking	Steganography (Denning, 1999): hiding a message in other data.
Repackaging	Computer virus hiding in an existing program such as a Trojan Horse.
Dazzling	Encryption, codes. Sending false messages to make believe something is being carried out when it is not.
Mimicking	Web page designed to look like the target's page.
Inventing	Virtual reality.
Decoying	Sending information so target directs effort to an activity beneficial to the attacker, for example by sending false market opportunities.

3.3 Digital deception

One major advantage of the digital media is the ability to easily manipulate the bits that constitute its messages. It is also one of its major disadvantages. For instance, the history of photographic manipulation[5] clearly shows the ease with which images can be changed to give a totally different perspective. In the digital realm, this is sold as one of the major advantages of computerised imagery. Photographic images, which were always slanted versions of reality, cannot even be taken to be that in today's digitised world. Any component of the image can be changed to reflect whatever is required. The power of visual imagery can be demonstrated[6]. Subtle changes can disproportionately change the meaning of an image. This is just as appropriate with simpler, conventional text messages. It can be imagined the damage caused to an organisation if a web-based employment advertisement phrase was changed from 'Applications from women especially welcome', to 'Applications from women not especially welcome'. This not so subtle change could easily cause the organisation involved an enormous amount of embarrassment with its inherent use of resources to rectify the situation. Exhibit 3.1 shows the ability to change data 'at a stroke'. The manipulation of this image took less than an hour. Can you trust any digital image to represent reality, or any text, or any figures ...?

Contemporary organisations with their reliance on information technology are vulnerable to deception. Of course, this technology also provides an opportunity. Each person or group can become a deceiver as well as being a victim of deception. Any management regime needs to be fully aware of the potential for deception, and its potential impact on organisation decision making and operations.

Information systems need to be trusted. Whilst information is a personal construct, the data needed to produce it should have high integrity. In other words, the data should be a true reflection of your world, and not that of a protagonist. On the other hand, you want the world of your protagonist to be yours. Hence, there is a defensive and offensive nature to digital information warfare.

Attacking the content, form of presentation, availability, and timeliness of data can cause deception to occur. However, if it is obvious the data has been attacked, points may have been scored in terms of inconvenience, but deception has not occurred. At its simplest, if a fraudster's attempt to alter financial data is intercepted in time then no deception has occurred.

For an example of an obvious web site attack, see exhibit 3.2. There may be some propaganda value here, but no real deception has occurred.

Exhibit 3.1: Which image is a real reflection of past events, or is either?

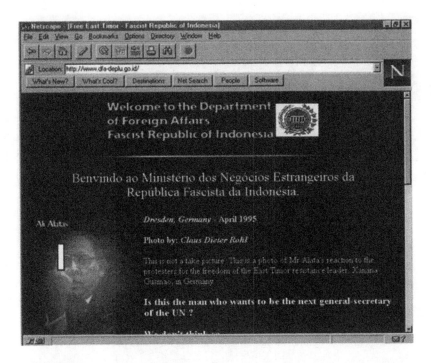

Exhibit 3.2: Indonesian web site after it had been attacked

The types of deception outlined in section 3.2 can now be applied to the digital world.

Masking (blending)

Here the aim is to make the data 'invisible' to the system rather like a well-camouflaged soldier in a thicket is to the naked eye. The event or object is there but the protagonist does not pick it up. Some computer viruses have the ability to merge into the system without being detected. Data can be hidden in other data but not recognised. For instance, in the process of steganography, extra data can be hidden in a digital image. Although the file holding the image and extra data is slightly larger, the image still appears the same when displayed. Unless the correct file size is known, the extra data (be it an executable file or not) may go unnoticed.

Masking the non-genuine transaction has been the aim of fraudsters for centuries. In the digital world, this means the non-detection of false transactions.

Repackaging (new wrapping)

This is similar to 'inventing' (see below) except that the point is not to create a new reality, but to dress the existing one. This new wrapping can be positive or negative. Organisations tend to give themselves a 'new wrapping' by exaggerating positive aspects of their operations, business success, staff morale, and so on. This 'clothing' that organisations wrap around themselves can be achieved by sending selected data to targeted recipients such as journalists. The reverse can occur, of course, if detrimental data is revealed about a target organisation. This 'public persona' of any organisation is important to help build the image received by the public, clients, government, and other stakeholders in the environment.

Dazzling (confusing the target)

This technique requires the target to be startled by the nature or quantity of the data presented. Encryption can cause 'confusion' to occur, as any attacker will not be able to read strongly encrypted data. An attacker can equally scramble data belonging to the target thereby making it unintelligible.

Bombarding a target with data can cause confusion. Sending of messages until the victim's system is saturated and paralysed is effective. Email 'bombing' is one such technique, but more inventive examples can include the false ordering of stock known to be in short supply, the over-supply of materials which cannot be sold or stored, or the overloading of a system by telephoning the victim's help desk *en masse*. Anything which sends the target's system into a panic is an illustration of this. This can be used as a disruption in its own right or as a diversion for another type of attack.

Mimicking (replicas)

An example of a mimicking approach is shown by exhibit 3.3. A web site pretending to represent the PKK (Partiya Karkeren Kurdistan – Kurdish Workers Party) actually represents an anti-PKK viewpoint.

This mimicking effect can be used to present the target in a

Exhibit 3.3: An example of a pro-PKK web site, or is it?

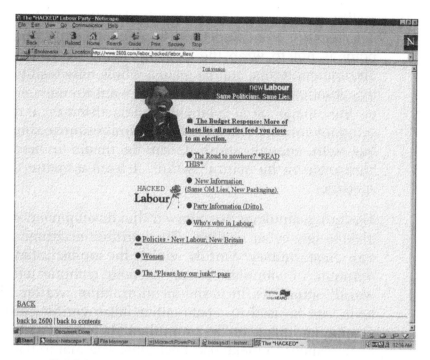

Exhibit 3.4: An attack on the British Labour Party site

particular way. It is often used to present the opposite political view held by the owners of the attacked site, or to
embarrass the victim. Exhibit 3.4 illustrates this with the
web page image of the British Labour Party site after an
attack.

Computer viruses often mimic other programs. A favourite
of hackers is 'social engineering' where they imitate
genuine system users or technical staff over the telephone
to obtain system data such as logon identification.

Inventing (new realities)

This is the world of such things as propaganda and advertising. Data and context are used to change the reality perceived by the intended audience. The target of the new

reality may be your own organisation (to give beneficial new reality), or a competitor (to give a negative one). The point is not to wrap the existing reality in beneficial or detrimental terms, but to create a whole **new** reality about the situation. An organisation may want to reinvent itself, or the image of a competitor. For instance, a mining company may be considered a 'natural resource company', but with enough effort it can be made to become a 'destroyer of the natural world'. It is all a matter of perspective.

Modern technology has allowed the development of completely new cyber realities. The world of electronic games can create fantasy worlds, whilst the sophisticated environment of simulation can recreate complicated 'real world' situations. In terms of information warfare, these tools can be used to create either false worlds causing a damaging image to be promulgated, or persuading its management to make bad decisions. The manipulation of images can create various impressions of the same situation. A telling comment about the Kosova war explains:

... the media creates an illusion that what we are seeing is true. In reality, nothing is what it seems. Atrocities are not necessarily atrocities. Victories are not necessarily victories. Damage is not necessarily collateral. But these deceptions have become intrinsic to the art of war. Virtual war is being won by being spun. In these circumstances, a good citizen is a highly suspicious one.[7]

Whilst this refers to war, it can also be relevant to any newsworthy corporate incident. In any event, it shows the potential effects of images and sounds that have been edited to produce a new reality. In I-War these manipulations should benefit the attacker. On the other hand, the victim should have contingency plans for such an attack. After the event reactions are usually not as effective as preemptive actions. Constant vigilance plus good intelligence followed by action can ameliorate some of the more predictable strikes.

Decoying (misdirection)

This technique, much loved by magicians, relies on a decoy allowing a misdirection of effort. For instance, exhibit 3.5 shows a web site which is displayed by mistyping a '0' (zero) for an 'o'. The site www.micros0ft.com is displayed. The error has caused another, probably unintended, mimic site to be obtained.

Data or presentations designed for decoying are intended to make the target expend effort in a direction to the benefit of the attacker and/or to the detriment of the victim. For

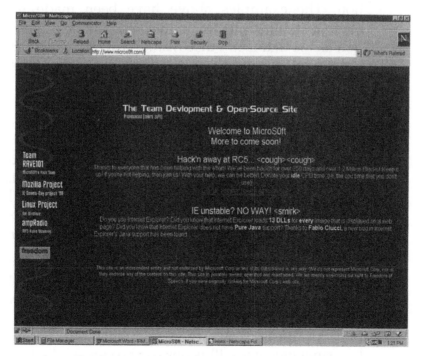

Exhibit 3.5: Web site www.micros0ft.com

example, data can be created giving false customer delivery details, or bogus requests for information. Even obvious and unsuccessful attempts at attacking a target's network can cause the expending of effort by network managers. This can possibly delay more critical tasks, and a misdirection of resources into unproductive areas. Decoy attacks thus produce the 'dazzling' effect mentioned previously.

At a more strategic level, false environmental data can be released referring to the market, industry trends, legal obligations, and other important issues upon which decisions, resource allocations, and effort are made.

The six types of deception provide a useful tool for the development of plans for deception. However, it is subtlety, imagination, and ingenuity that create good deception. The examples above have been made relatively obvious to illustrate the points being made. A good deception is one that is not discovered. A weak deception can be used to cover a stronger one: the more cunning the strategy taken, the better the effect.

3.4 Deception by changing presentation of data

The aim of deception is to create an illusion to convey a message which distorts reality. Whilst changing data can lead to this, so can the way it is presented. Also, the data may have the same values but the timing, or the medium by which it is presented, can affect its interpretation.

For instance, the fairly basic environment of email is prone to successful deceptive activities. It is an emotionally cold world devoid of body language signals (a major indicator of lying), and has few visual or auditory cues. Text often appears abrupt. However, if emotional intelligence is used to format messages, illusions can be created. Male message senders can become female, the powerless can become important, the meek strong. In fact, you can become whatever you want. Even the email address can be used to convey messages. The username 'dr.smith' sends a different message to one named 'ravenous'. Domain names indicate academia (.edu, or .ac), government (.gov), commercial (.com), and so on. Countries of origin can (apparently!) be ascertained (for example, .uk, .au, .nz). A whole image of the sender can be built by the message receiver … but is it real?

In fact, human psychology shows:

Our own stereotypes about how certain people should behave will also trigger suspicions about truthfulness and deception on the Internet. These will be primitive, indeed, but … we are cognitive misers and use stereotypes and categories routinely to save time. For better or worse, we expect people to act in predictable ways, given the age, sex, occupation, race, or status.[8]

Any message sent to deceive should take this into account.

Certain characteristics within text give cues for truthfulness. Truthful messages tend to be complete, direct, relevant, clear, and personalised. If these are the signs people are looking for, then a false message should use them to add credibility.

Creating an illusion can be incredibly easy. In a recent exercise, the web site of a health authority was accessed and the logo copied. A letter using it was then created using medical technology warning of an outbreak of a serious contagious disease. A 'help desk' telephone number was also supplied for further information, where someone could answer any questions even though the number was bogus. Other details to add to the illusion were created. The exercise went no further but the amount of panic and disruption that could have been caused by this being faxed to all hospital administrators can be guessed. Using this principle in other spheres requires only a little imagination. The multimedia environment is less restrictive than plain text but is still not always interactive, and mostly visual and auditory rather than tactile or olfactory. The clever use of colour, shade, scale, thickness of lines, and voice to create impressions will add to any illusion.

Presentation of data can often be much more important than the actual content. Points can be emphasised or de-emphasised. Smiles can become grimaces, spots become smooth skin, a graph's slope can become steeper, a voice threatening or inviting, and a piece of text highlighted or not.

3.5 Some principles for creating an illusion

Mental models

The human brain controls our perception of the world. The internal workings of this complicated mechanism produce models of the world, which enable us to digest the myriad of data thrown at our senses. These models developed by experience, socialisation, ability, culture, biology, and technology allow us to survive. Of course, there are drawbacks. Each of us has different models, and each person develops biases. These biases give us many illusory effects. Most people are aware of externally created effects such as visual illusions[9] (see figures 3.2 and 3.3), but many are not so conscious of the more abstract and internally constructed cognitive illusions[10]. At least, they are not conscious of their own. Those wishing to deceive can exploit these illusory effects.

Filling in the gaps

Figure 3.2 is a simple example of how we take a minimal amount of data and interpret it according to our precon-

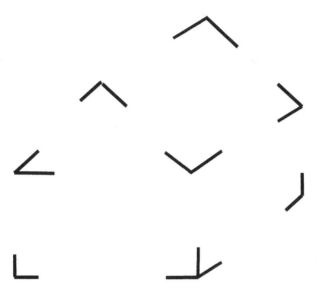

Figure 3.2: 'Knowing' with incomplete information

ceived mental models. For those brought up in a society whose dominant buildings were circular, the diagram might represent a badly drawn set of joined lines with no apparent meaning. However, most of us 'know' that the figure represents a house. Hence by feeding people bits of data, mental models can be used to create illusions which suit the initiator. Each one of the pieces means nothing by itself, but given the correct context 2+2 can equal 45! All that is needed is the desired end result, the context, and the correct pieces of data to build a house out of 17 short and badly drawn lines.

Relying on bias

Figure 3.3 illustrates the persistence of our mental models. No amount of measuring will allow us to see the two horizontal lines as the same length (actually, the lower one is slightly longer). Again, our rational self 'knows' the length

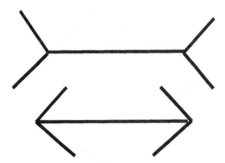

Figure 3.3: Mental models overcome reality

of the lines as we can measure them, but our brain cannot 'see' it. Our in-built biases and prejudices make us very prone to being led down paths others want us to follow if data is fed to us which reinforces these models. Give the data the people want! Expert hackers using social engineering use this principle to fool others that they are other than they actually are. Sensitive information can then be obtained. Give the target data and let them fill in the holes by exploiting their own preconceptions about the world.

Our cognitive models play tricks with our thoughts. Examples are attitudes toward the often anti-intuitive nature of probability theory, and our lack of acceptance of the statistically provable, for our trust in an irrational and erroneous position. For example, take the details of a certain person. X is intelligent, not particularly creative, good at mathematics, very much a loner, loves computer games, and is 19 years of age. Now, from the options below, order them by the probability of each statement about X being true (do this before reading the next paragraph):

♦ X is a marketing manager.

♦ X is a professional computer programmer.

♦ X loves ballroom dancing.

- X is a computer hacker.

- X is a nurse.

- X is a professional computer programmer and a hacker.

- X is a marketing manager who also likes ballroom dancing.

From the very scant information you were given, did you decide the person X was a male or female? Did you assume X was a computer programmer? Did you put the option that X is a 'professional computer programmer and a hacker' before the single options of 'professional computer programmer' or 'computer hacker'. The latter mistake is very common, although a cursory knowledge of statistics would let you realise that the probability of someone being both options is always less than a person being one of them (unless one option has a probability of 1).

The point of the above example is that a person's biases can be exploited by feeding data which reinforces the image wanted. Another point is that, in this case, the author also set the context (a very powerful tactic). A boundary was drawn around X and only the options the author wanted you to think about were presented. Of course, we do this every day of our lives just to survive. A good example of this tactic can be given by the case of a clever committee member listing out options for an agenda item. If those options are passed around the table (or a computerised version of the table!), the conversation normally revolves around them. The options presented set the context of further discussion. As most members have done little preparation, the prepared list makes the problem easier for them and so guides the outcome. Restricting the set of input data influences the output information.

The previous section has briefly described some principles of deception in action. In summary, they are:

- ♦ Provide data you want others to know.

- ♦ Provide data which sets the context for your aims.

- ♦ Provide data which develops biases of the target in your favour.

- ♦ It is not necessary to provide all the data but just enough for the target to 'join the dots'.

Do not believe all you believe!

3.6 Why lie?

As deception is a conscious activity, it can be assumed that it requires some form of motive. Ford[11] gives some insight into the types of lies and their associated motives. Whilst his analysis is related to individuals, the classification can profitably be used with organisations. Table 3.4 summarises Ford's findings with the authors' additions for organisational motives.

Table 3.4 shows both sides of an organisation's motives to lie both to protect itself and to compromise an 'enemy' or competitor. Organisational deceptions can be used to promote its image (the conventional public relations function), to discredit its competitors (an activity rarely admitted), or to gain advantage by other methods.

The act of lying is rarely admitted in organisations. The distinction between lying and such activities as advertising is also blurred. Perhaps the more neutral phrase perception management provides a vehicle to carry out meaningful dialogue in this area. In competitive organisational environments, it has always been a potential strategy to deceive competitors, regulators, clients, and even suppliers. It should be the aim of an organisation to ensure that it is in control of its image, not others. However, as table 3.4

shows there are no shortages of reasons to deceive at the organisational level.

Table 3.4: Types of lies and motives for using them

Type of lie	Individual's motive	Possible organisational attacker's motive
Benign and salutary lies	To affect social conventions	To affect or destroy a good corporate public image
Hysterical lies	To attract attention	To attract attention
Defensive lies	To extricate oneself from a difficult situation	To extricate an organisation from a difficult legal/corporate image situation (or to involve a victim in one)
Compensatory lies	To impress other people	To impress clients, the public, etc.
Malicious lies	To deceive for personal gain	To obtain market share or fraud
Gossip	To exaggerate rumours maliciously	To compromise a competitor
Implied lies	To mislead by partial truths	Disinformation to protect/harm an organisation
'Love intoxication' lies	To exaggerate idealistically	To promote/discredit an organisation
Pathological lies	To lie self-destructively	Unusual, possibly to lower the value of a company for buy-out, etc.

3.7 The surveillance society

Modern western society is one where surveillance is constant. Traffic is monitored, vehicle number plates and faces recognised and checked, emails/telephone calls logged and audited, shopping and bank account transactions stored, analysed, and profiles created. Cameras watch some workplaces, and individual productivity rates are scrutinised in real time. Road haulage trucks, ambulances, and police cars are tracked by satellite positioning. Their exact position now and in the past can be established. There is a mountain of data about every facet of our lives. Both individuals and corporations cannot hide, or can they? The naïve argument, which says, 'I have nothing to hide. I do not mind anyone knowing', to which the reply is 'Good. Could you please tell me all about your profits, income, sex life, sexual preferences, conviction history, etc.', is dismissed here. There are many issues concerning privacy, misuse of data, and power disparities caused by data ownership raised by increasing, and seemingly uncontrolled, surveillance. The use of surveillance in almost all areas of society may make deception the only real defence against government, corporate, and individual snooping in the future. The technology of surveillance from satellite imagery to miniature cameras is too widespread to be rid of it; it is only illusion that can be effective against it.

Notes

1 See Howard, M. (1990) *Strategic Deception in the Second World War*, W.W. Norton & Co. Ltd, London.

2 This table is based on an idea by Wickens (1992) in the area of Signal Detection Theory. See Wickens, C.D. (1992) *Engineering Technology and Human Performance*, Addison-Wesley.

3 See: Heuer, R.J. (1999) *Psychology of Intelligence Analysis*, Centre for the Study of Intelligence, Central Intelligence Agency, USA p. 3.

4 The concepts presented here are derived from Bowyer, J.B. (1982) *Cheating*, St Martin's Press, New York.

5 See Roberts, P., Webber, J. (1999) Visual Truth in the Digital Age: Towards a Protocol for Image Ethics, *Australian Computer Journal*, **31**:3, 78–82.

[6] See Barry, A.M.S. (1997) *Visual Intelligence*, State University of New York Press.

[7] This quote comes from Ignatieff, M. (2000) *Virtual War*, Chatto & Windus, London, p. 196.

[8] This quote comes from Wallace, P. (1999) *The Psychology of the Internet*, Cambridge University Press, Cambridge, pp. 52–53. Other ideas in this section are also derived from this text.

[9] See Robinson, J.O. (1998) *The Psychology of Visual Illusion*, Dover Publications, New York, for a fuller description of visual illusions.

[10] See Piattelli-Palmarini, M. (1994) *Inevitable Illusions*, John Wiley and Sons, New York, for a comprehensive discussion of cognitive illusions.

[11] See Ford, C.V. (1996) *Lies! Lies!! Lies!!! The Psychology of Deceit*, American Psychiatric Press, Washington.

4 | Sources of threat for IT systems

4.1 Attack

I-War attacks are focused upon attacking a country's National Information Infrastructure (NII). The NII reflects the collective computer systems that make up the computerised military, government, commercial and educational information systems of a country. A new aspect of information warfare is the fact that electronic commerce (e-commerce) is developing into a key area of the commercial part of the NII. E-commerce sites represent easy targets to would-be attackers. Security is usually not as tight as in secured military systems, and these systems tend to be always on-line via the Internet. Any damage to these systems creates publicity for the attackers and losses to the businesses concerned (either through physical damage, credibility, or financial loss). Many organisations do not consider the security risks when developing on-line services.

Within the USA national security surveys[1] have shown that 20% of US organisations have experienced attacks against their e-commerce applications. The main types of attacks are:

♦ Vandalism
♦ Financial fraud
♦ Denial of service
♦ Theft of transaction information

Deception can be applied to all of these attack scenarios. This then becomes a worrying trend as e-commerce grows and develops as a major part of the commercial NII.

4.2 Methods of attack

There are a number of commonly used techniques that can be employed to attack computer systems that form part of a country's NII.

Password cracking

This is one of the simplest and most common methods of attack, using software packages such as Brute (PC based), Passfinder (Mac based), Crack V4.1 (Unix based) to obtain computer passwords. These packages run in a number of ways, e.g. accessing a system via a File Transfer Protocol (FTP) port and trying to determine password files. Another method is to use software that systematically uses a combination of passwords until one is successful. There are even now companies that offer a password cracking service. These types of attacks could damage an organisation's information systems in a number of ways. For example, unauthorised access could allow the attacker to:

♦ delete, or change data relating to orders, pricing, or product description;

♦ copy data for use by a competitor for fraudulent purposes.

Spoofing attacks

IP (Internet Protocol) spoofing was first associated with the hacker Kevin Mitnick[2] and his attacks on networks. It works by forging the 'From' address so that the message appears to have originated from somewhere other than its actual source. Normally, the false address is that of a site, which is trusted by the receiving host, so that the packet will be accepted and acted upon, in some cases allowing an intruder to penetrate right through a firewall[3]. Another type of spoofing is known as web spoofing. This is where an attacker sets up a fake web site to lure users in hopes of stealing information such as their credit card numbers. One hacker group set up a site called micros0ft.com, using the number zero in place of the letter 'o', which many users might type by mistake (see exhibit 4.1). Users might find themselves in a situation where they do not notice they are using a bogus web site and give their credit card details.

An attacker may use these techniques in a number of ways, for example cracking passwords and setting up false web sites with the intent to defraud, thus raising funds or creat-

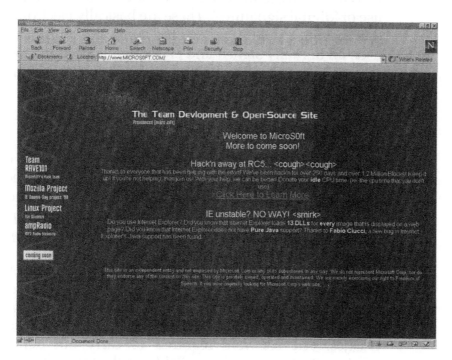

Exhibit 4.1: Example of www.micros0ft.com

ing misinformation, for example pretending the web site is an official supplier. The disruption that these attacks cause would be different to other forms of attack. Since the user of such a site would think they are using an official site they would disclose information relating to their password, customer number, order and credit card details, etc. This information could be used later to access the official on-line service and masquerade as a customer and make false orders, credit card details could be used in other fraudulent activities.

It is possible to protect against bogus web sites. The Secure Sockets Layer tool that comes packaged with most web browsers cannot determine a fake web site. The way to overcome this problem is to add authentication software between the client and server so that the client can be sure it is connecting to the correct web site. An alternative is the use of 'digital signatures'. These are basically electronic IDs that include a public key and the name and address of the user, all digitally signed and encrypted with a private key. These IDs are proof of identity and that a message has not been tampered with.

Denial-of-service attacks

A denial-of-service attack occurs when access to a computer or network resource is intentionally blocked or degraded as a result of malicious action taken by another user. These attacks do not necessarily damage data directly or permanently (although they could), but they intentionally compromise the availability of the resources. They tend to affect the availability of computer systems for legitimate usage. These forms of attacks can include email bomb attacks, systemically sending thousands of emails to a particular computer system email server until that server crashes. The software required to carry out denial-of-service attacks is widely available on the Internet.

Another commonly used denial-of-service attack is the Ping O'Death ('ping' messages are used to determine whether another machine on a network is active). The Ping O'Death can crash or reboot a computer by sending a 'ping' message of greater than 65 536 bytes – the default size is 64 Kbytes. Router updates have nearly eliminated these problems. Attackers with a low level of expertise would commonly carry out these sorts of attacks. The reason for this is that they require a very low technical skill level, and the software is freely available on the Internet. Denial-of-service attacks could be very effective against an internet based company, since they rely on on-line connectivity. They can be very effective in disrupting the on-line mechanisms used with the electronic commerce process. The impact of the attacks can be twofold: causing the system to crash which means that suppliers cannot access the on-line service, or sending so many false email messages to an organisation that it would take hours to delete them and determine which messages were authentic.

Direct attack

A direct attack would take the form of hacking into a computer system and rewriting or stealing information. This would have a great impact on organisations offering on-line services, since they could be damaged, modified or destroyed. Another problem is that if the organisation were not able to determine where the security risk lies, the direct attacks can be recurring. The impact of these attacks could be to publicise the attackers and destroy the creditability of the organisation offering the on-line services especially to current and future customers. We have also seen that certain types of organisations have already been victims of these types of attacks. For instance, hackers have attacked large music companies' on-line sites in order to get their message to the general public (as shown by exhibit 4.2) and disrupt the on-line services offered by the record company.

Another method of hacking is more concerned with attacking computer files and destroying, modifying or extracting data. These types of hacking attacks may be less apparent to organisations, as they may not realise they have been a victim. Attackers would use direct hacking as an extensive part of their 'attack strategy' against e-commerce. By hacking web sites they will gain a global audience for their actions and will also be able to discredit the security of the companies using the on-line services.

These types of attacks could damage an organisation's e-commerce functionality in a number of ways. For example, suppliers would not be able to access the on-line system until it is restored. Another impact is the adverse publicity

Exhibit 4.2: Successful hack of a large music company

caused for the organisation targeted.

Research within Australia has shown that the main concern that users have about e-commerce applications is security[4]. This means that direct attacks on e-commerce systems could cause some initial damage but, more much importantly, could destroy customer confidence in such systems.

Viruses

The term 'virus' is a general term for a program that infects a computer by copying itself onto the hard disk. Some damage data, others files, or the hard disk. They tend to attack executable program files, the file directory, the boot system, or data files. There are different types such as 'Trojan Horses' (these disguise themselves as normal programs), and 'Worms' (these are designed to infect networks, and travel from computer to computer replicating themselves on the way).

A new trend in the development of viruses is the development of Microsoft Office macro viruses these are viruses specifically written in the macro language of Microsoft products such as Word, Excel and Access. These style of viruses are spread quickly via the use of email.

An example of a macro virus is the 'Love Bug' virus let loose in the year 2000. This focused upon Microsoft's Outlook product. The virus is email Macro virus. This means that in order for the virus to be run the user must double click the attachment on the email. The attachment is entitled *'LOVE-LETTER-FOR-YOU.TXT.vbs'*. After the user clicks the attachment, the macro script becomes enabled. The first thing it does is to save itself to three different locations. Then it creates several start-up commands to execute the programs when the machine restarts. A worm also modifies Internet Explorer's start page to randomly select between four URLs at the domain www.skyinet.net that will download a program. The virus then changes some registry keys in order to run the down-loaded program, this program will also email information found in the cache to a Philippine email account.

If the user is using Microsoft Outlook, the virus will access the address book and send an email with an attachment called '*LOVE-LETTER-FOR-YOU.TXT.vbs*'. The text of the mail starts out by saying: 'kindly check the attached LOVELETTER coming from me' to all email addresses in that address book. The worm then searches for attached drives containing files with certain extensions, and pro-ceeds to rename the files with different file extensions. The virus then creates an HTML file and floods any chat chan-nels with the '*LOVE-LETTER-FOR-YOU.HTML*' file to anyone who joins a chat with the user.

The fact that this virus utilised an attack method focusing upon Microsoft Outlook meant that it was spread very quickly. From an initial starting point in Asia it quickly spread around the globe. Financial losses due to the 'Love Bug' virus are estimated to have reached about US$10 billion.

The virus was tracked to the Philippines and authorities arrested a computer student.

4.3 Steps to reduce risks

The biggest step that can be taken to reduce the risks asso-ciated with I-War is awareness. Many governments are undertaking research into this area. Extensive Australian government research has been undertaken in the area of computer security risk reduction[5]. The study found that areas in which organisations can reduce risks are:

♦ organisations should implement protective security measures such as passwords, access control, encryption in accordance to a defined security standard such as BS7799[6];

♦ organisations should formally accredit themselves against security standards;

♦ organisations should raise awareness of security issues and e-commerce risks among their staff;

♦ organisations should train their staff in how to use computer security systems efficiently and effectively.

Research into organisational security has identified some key factors to be considered by companies to reduce their security risks. Organisations could improve the risks associated with their system by focusing on[7]:

Technical interventions

Technological advances in the form of on-line response systems (for example, what is your mother's maiden name?) have helped in securing information assets by implementing levels of access control system based upon users' prior knowledge. However, an over-reliance on technology seems to present a false sense of security.

Formal interventions

Formal interventions pertain to reorienting information and security practices around a reorganised structure. If an organisation has created new processes for conducting its business, then adequate emphasis needs to be placed on developing controls and rules that reflect the emergent structure. Usually security and formal controls are considered as an 'afterthought' – when something goes wrong.

The measures should be an integral part of the system design, not just an implementation factor.

Informal interventions

Increasing awareness of security issues is cost effective. It is often the case that IT security is presented to the users in a form that is beyond their comprehension. Hence, it becomes a demotivating factor in implementing adequate controls. Increased awareness should be supplemented with an ongoing education and training programme.

These approaches highlight the areas of weakness of security within traditional organisations. The area of e-commerce security is a very complex issue, and combined with the complexities of e-commerce misuse, the problem becomes an even greater issue. Perhaps we are beginning to see the limitations of computer security technologies.

4.4 Conclusion

We are now facing a situation where individual countries' NIIs are being developed. There are now a variety of attack methods that can be used to attack a country's NII. Only time will tell whether e-commerce is the weak link in many NIIs.

Notes

[1] Details can be found in CSI/FBI (1999) *Computer Crime and Security Survey*, Computer Security Institute, USA.

[2] Details can be found in Littman, J. (1997) *The Watchman – The Twisted Life and Crimes of Serial Hacker Kevin Poulsen*, Little, Brown & Company Limited, USA, ISBN 0-316-52857-9.

[3] Details can be found in Denning, D.E. (1999) *Information Warfare and Security*, Addison-Wesley, New York.

4 Details can be found in DIST (Department of Industry, Science and Tourism). (1998) *Stats – Electronic Commerce in Australia*, Commonwealth of Australia, Australia.

5 Details can be found in Attorney-General's Department (1998) *Protecting Australia's National Information Infrastructure*, Report of the Interdepartmental Committee on Protection of the National Information Infrastructure, Attorney-General's Department, Canberra, Australia.

6 Other standards such as the Australia/New Zealand AS/NZS 4444 exist and are equivalent to the UK's BS 7799 standard.

7 Details relate to Dhillon, G. (1999) Managing and controlling computer misuse. *Information Management & Computer Security*, Vol. 7, No. 5.

5 | Attacks and retaliation

5.1 Source of attack

Within this section we will look at who carries out I-War attacks. Many aspects of our modern society now have either a direct or implicit dependence upon information technology (IT). As such, a compromise of the availability or integrity of these systems (which may encompass such diverse domains as banking, government, healthcare and law enforcement) could have dramatic consequences socially.

In many modern business environments, even a short-term, temporary interruption of internet or email connectivity can have a significant disruptive effect, forcing people to revert to other forms of communication that are now viewed as less convenient. Imagine then the effect if the denial of service was over the longer term and also affected the IT infrastructure in general. Many governments are now coming to this realisation. We therefore have to consider the scenario in which technology infrastructures or services are targeted deliberately, examining the issue in relation to two categories of computer abuser: 'hackers' and 'cyber terrorists/criminals'.

The definition of the 'computer hacker' has been the subject of much debate in computing circles. Research[1] has provide two definitions of the term:

1. In programming, a computing enthusiast. The term is normally applied to people who take a delight in experimenting with system hardware (the electronics), soft-

ware (computer programs) and communication systems (telephone lines, in most cases).

2. In data (information) security, an unauthorised user who tries to gain entry into a computer, or computer network, by defeating the computer's access (and/or security) controls.

In mass media terms, the latter interpretation is by far the more common, although persons belonging to the former category of hacker would seek to more accurately define the latter group, particularly those with a malicious intent, as 'crackers'.

Hackers are by no means a new threat and have routinely featured in news stories during the last two decades. Indeed, they have become the traditional 'target' of the media, with the standard approach being to present the image of either a 'teenage whiz-kid' or an insidious threat. In reality, it can be argued that there are different degrees of the problem. Some hackers are malicious, whilst others are merely naïve and, hence, do not appreciate that their activities may be doing any real harm. Furthermore, when viewed as a general population, hackers may be seen to have numerous motivations for their actions, including financial gain, revenge, ideology or just plain mischief making. However, in many cases it can be argued that this is immaterial as, no matter what the reason, the end result has some form of adverse impact upon another party.

A series of surveys concerned about all forms of IT abuse have been conducted by the UK Audit Commission[2]. They considered various types of incident (including hacking, viruses, fraud, sabotage and theft) across a number of industries and sectors including government, healthcare, banking, retail and education. They recorded the consequences of the incidents in terms of financial losses which may have occurred, directly or indirectly, as a result of the incidents. Also, it is likely that other, less measurable, consequences may also have occurred as a result, for example disruption to operations, breaches of personal privacy or commercial confidentiality, etc. Similar research from around the world also shows the extent of the problem. The US national surveys[3] showed that 51% of the total number of respondents acknowledged losses due to IT abuse. However, only 31% could quantify the damage. Nevertheless losses amounted to US$124 million.

In recent years there has been widespread use of information technology by terrorist-type organisations. This has led to the emergence of a new class of threat, which has been termed cyber terrorism. This can be viewed as distinct from 'traditional' terrorism since physical terror does not occur and efforts are instead focused upon attacking information systems or resources. When viewed from the perspective of skills and techniques, there is little to distinguish cyber terrorists from the general classification of hackers; both groups require and utilise an arsenal of techniques in order to breach the security of target systems. From a motivational perspective, however, cyber terrorists are clearly different, operating with a specific political or ideological agenda to support their actions. This in turn may result in more focused and determined efforts to achieve their objectives and more considered selection of suitable targets to attack. The difference, however, does not necessarily end there and other factors should be considered. Firstly, the fact that cyber terrorists are part of an organised group could mean that they have funding and resources available to support their activities. This in turn would mean that individual hackers could be hired to carry out attacks on behalf of a terrorist organisation (effectively subcontracting the necessary technical expertise). In this situation, the hackers themselves may not believe in the terrorist's 'cause', but will undertake the work for financial gain.

The real threat in the 'cyber' context is when the Internet (or the more general technological infrastructure) becomes the medium in which a terrorist-type attack is conducted. In this sense, it is somewhat ironic that the Internet, which was originally conceived as a means of ensuring continued communications in the event of a nuclear war destroying the conventional telecommunications infrastructure, should now itself represent a medium through which widespread damage can be caused to the new information society. It is possible to view technology as some kind of 'great equaliser' between major countries and governments and smaller groups. This is a battlefield where success relies upon intellectual skills and software creativity as opposed to sheer volume and physical resources. In short, the individuals or small groups may, in theory, have as much chance of succeeding as a superpower. To see the potential for damage, you only have to look at the results of actions from individuals who have acted without a war motive and without government or official backing. Consider the impact that computer hacking and virus incidents have had upon businesses in recent years. The most significant threats come from the integrity and availability aspects. Security breaches in these respects have the potential to do the most direct damage, for example by making systems unavailable or having them operate on the basis of incorrect data. Breaches of confidentiality could, however, have an indirect value in a terrorism or warfare context but have a major propaganda impact for the terrorists' cause. Attacks can also occur from 'legitimate' sources such as traditional governments, for all of the reasons explained above.

Exhibit 5.1 is an example of where anti-government forces used the Internet as a means of supporting their actions in overthrowing a democratically elected government.

Exhibit 5.1: Official Pakistani Government web page hacked by Pakistani
military supporters

5.2 Retaliation

There are two approaches organisations can take towards I-War and attackers. They can be defined as being passive or aggressive responses.

Passive response

The passive response in I-War is based upon developing a form of perimeter security and trying to defend it against possible on-line security attacks. This traditional approach is based upon developing firewalls to protect the organisation's computer assets against unauthorised external access. Companies also maintain their perimeter defence by conducting security analysis reviews to determine possible threats, and then strengthen security by implementing additional countermeasures and developing policies to make sure staff are aware of their security duties.

The problem with style of response is that an organisation only reacts once they have been attacked. If the attack was aimed at a particular security weakness that was unknown internally, the attacker would be able to gain access and cause damage. It is then left to the organisation to upgrade the security weakness after the damage has been done.

This is one of the reasons why the FIRST (Forum of Incident Response and Security Teams) was set up. They were to supply organisations with information so that they could update their security protection before an attack took place.

FIRST[4] is an international consortium of computer incident response and security teams who work together to handle computer security incidents and to promote preventive activities. The mission of FIRST is to:

♦ provide members with technical information, tools, methods, assistance, and guidance;

♦ co-ordinate proactive liaison activities and analytical support;

♦ encourage the development of quality products and services;

♦ improve national and international information security for government, private industry, academia and the individual;

♦ enhance the image and status of the incident response and security teams (IRST) community in the outside world.

As long as organisations are warned about new security

threats or weaknesses they can upgrade their security mechanisms, but without that information they face attacks from unknown assailants.

Aggressive response

The concept of retaliation to an information attack must be considered in relation to the benefits to the organisation. One motivation may be 'vengeance'. However, this personal and subjective rationale has no meaning in organisational terms unless it is coupled with 'deterrence'. The idea that any attacker who can be identified will be subjected to the same sort of aggression might be a deterrent to that particular attacker and others in general. However, as many of the comments below indicate, it might be a trigger to some attackers to re-attack. Hence, a vicious cycle of attack and retaliation may develop. This is not the stuff of rational management, although in many competitive environments it is present.

Another major inhibitor to vigilante practices is that of legal liability and public relations. Hacking a hacker puts the organisation in the same legal position as the original attacker. Whilst the chance of getting prosecuted may be the same, the likely financial penalties may not. The chance of destroying equipment and/or data of an innocent whose address has been used illegally might be a public relations nightmare if an organisation were caught.

A recent I-War text[5] states, '... the goal of Information Warfare is not to symbolically "kill" the intruder but to fend off his every attempt to penetrate the system'. This implies a dynamic but reactive (rather than proactive) approach. However, this approach is the very reason why the attacker might always hold the initiative.

Attacks on the systems can have positive outcomes. The

lessons learned about security weaknesses can make the protective system much more effective. Keeping the potential for aggressive attack in the forefront of security management can also revitalise such things as access monitoring.

Recent events in Australia have increased the scope of aggressive responses to I-War attacks. The Australian Security Intelligence Organisation (ASIO) has received approval to hack into personal computers and bug on-line communications under new legislation[6]. The Australian Security Intelligence Organisation Legislation Amendment Bill 1999 (Parliament of the Commonwealth of Australia, 1999) gives ASIO a range of new powers authorising its officers to:

♦ use a computer or other electronic equipment found on a subject's premises to access computer data relevant to national security;

♦ copy, add, delete or alter data in computers or other electronic equipment;

♦ modify protection mechanisms in a computer or other electronic equipment;

♦ obtain remote access to data held in a computer;

♦ undertake anything reasonably necessary to conceal the fact that anything has been done by ASIO officers.

This range of new powers will allow the ASIO to engage in offensive on-line activities to protect the 'national interest' of Australia. Similar provisions have been made in the UK, Europe, and the USA. It brings into question any evidence from an electronic source presented in court. Who can trust that it has not been tampered with?

National response

Because of the complexity of I-War and defending a country's NII, the role of government becomes paramount. In the USA, a special presidential commission was set up to evaluate attacks upon America's NII. The commission determined:

Our dependence on the information and communications infrastructure has created new cyber vulnerabilities, which we are only starting to understand. In addition to the disruption of information and communications, we also face the possibility that someone will be able to actually mount an attack against other infrastructures by exploiting their dependence on computers and telecommunications[7].

The report led to the establishment of the National Infrastructure Protection Centre (NIPC)[8]. This is a US$64 million facility, employing some 500 staff across the country, with representatives taken from existing agencies such as the Secret Service, the CIA, NASA, the National Security Agency, the Department of Defense and several others. The role of NIPC is to 'detect, deter, assess, warn of, respond to, and investigate computer intrusions and unlawful acts' that threaten or target US critical infrastructures such as telecommunications, energy, banking and finance, water systems, government operations and emergency services.

We are now seeing a situation where governments are starting to protect the NII and also give advice to organisations on how they can protect their computer assets.

5.3   Conclusion

Whether we find it acceptable or not, modern society has a significant (and increasing) dependence upon information technology. Because of this dependence, the impact of hackers can be significant. However, the threats are still perceived by managers to come from individuals, whereas more significant dangers may come from organised groups. We face a number of immediate and long-term threats that need to be recognised in order for protective action to be taken. But who should take this action?

Notes

[1] Caelli, W., Longley, D. and Shain, M. (1989) *Information Security for Managers*, Stockton Press, New York.

[2] Audit Commission (1990) *Survey of Computer Fraud & Abuse*, UK. Audit Commission (1994) *Opportunity Makes a Thief: An Analysis of Computer Abuse*, UK. Audit Commission (1998) *Ghost in the Machine – An Analysis of IT Fraud and Abuse*, UK.

[3] CSI/FBI (1999) *Computer Crime and Security Survey*, Computer Security Institute, USA.

[4] See URL: www.first.org

[5] Forno, R., Baklarz R. (1999) *The Art of Information Warfare* – second edition, Universal Publishers.

[6] Tebbutt, D. (1999) Australia: Canberra Gives Spies Hack Power. *The Australian* (30/11/1999).

[7] See URL: www.ciao.gov/PCCIP/PCCIP_index.htm

[8] See URL: www.nipc.gov

6 | Attack and defence

6.1   The scenario

The world has seen the first I-War attacks. They have been numerous, and some examples are given below. What happened, and could they have been prevented?

Events

At about 1.15pm on Monday, 7 February 2000, Yahoo was hit by a DDoS (Distributed Denial of Service) attack from over 50 different locations on the Internet. At the height of the attack Yahoo was flooded with one gigabit of traffic a second. This is more than most sites receive in a year[1]. This continued until 4.25pm, and Yahoo's popular sites *yahoo.com*, *broadcast.com*, and *my.yahoo.com* were unreachable. Initially, some of the network engineers thought the problem was due to misconfigured equipment but soon a Yahoo spokesperson announced they were under a 'co-ordinated distributed denial-of-service attack'[2].

On Tuesday, 8 February at 1.50pm, *buy.com*, an on-line discount retailer, was struck by a DDoS attack receiving 800 megabits of data a second, some 24 times the normal flow[3]. The attack continued until about 5pm, and on the very same day *buy.com* went public. The company stocks which opened at $27 and traded as high as $35, closed at a disappointing $25 after the news of the disruption had reached the market[4]. At 5.45pm that day, on-line auction site *eBay.com* was disabled for more than two hours. At 7pm, *CNN.com* was attacked at the same time they were carrying the story of the attacks on other sites. At 8pm on-line bookstore *amazon.com* was the next victim, being unreachable for many users for about an hour.

On Wednesday, 9 February, further sites were hit. Firstly, *Zdnet.com* followed by on-line broker *e*Trade*[1]. Microsoft's *MSN.com* was also affected, apparently indirectly, because of the disruptions to several of the Internet Service Providers carrying its traffic. In later days it emerged that *Excite@Home* and some other major sites, which were not publicly identified out of fear of an adverse public reaction, were also affected on Wednesday[4].

The cost

While most of the effected web sites tried to put a brave face on the effect of the attacks, the Yankee Group, an information technology consulting and industry research company, estimated the attacks cost US$1.2 billion.

The attack resulted in capitalization losses that exceeded $1 billion on the days of the attacks. Revenue loss, both sales and advertisement revenue, is expected to exceed $100 million. Subsequently, the Yankee Group believes that the affected companies and their Internet peers will spend an additional $100–$200 million on security infrastructure upgrades in excess of what was already slated for fiscal year 2000. The resulting brand image, partnership, and future customer damage will result in further significant damage to all of these companies[5].

eBay's president and chief executive Meg Whitman claimed that they had not lost any revenue just US$80 000 in new expenses[6]. Greg Hawkins, chief executive of *buy.com*, said, 'We have clearly lost revenue', because of the attack occurring on their initial public offering. While there is some dispute as to the exact figure there is no doubt the cost of the attacks was considerable.

Could it have been prevented?

Perhaps one of the most surprising aspect of the attacks was that there had been many warnings about the DDoS tools, and their likely effects, before the attack. CERT advisories had been distributed about DDoS tools[7]. Even one of the victims of the attacks, ZDnet, carried a story on DDoS tools on 6 December 1999 on its ZDTV site. The story quotes Christopher Klaus of Internet Security Systems who stated in their article:

This marks a new step evolution of computer crime and sophistication of hacker tools and what people are doing to commit attacks on the Internet.[8]

Despite this, ZDnet and other sites were caught short when the attack came. What preventive measures could have been implemented given these prior warnings? Part of the problem was with the hosts used as agents in the attack and the administrators of those systems. Information was available for them to detect the problem on their systems if they had been more attentive.

What is the liability of these organisations to those disabled and who suffered losses in the attacks[9]? Did their executives show due diligence in performing vulnerability assessments? The problem is that in practice there will always be vulnerable sites as the Internet grows and the average experience level of administrators and managers decreases. This means the potential for overlooking security alerts, patches that should be installed, and unusual activity on a network, is even greater.

The sites attacked could have done a number of things to reduce the effect of the attacks. Filtering out all ICMP (*Internet Control Message Protocol*) packets as Yahoo did is one way. However, this is only a short-term measure that can be applied once you know you are affected by a Smurf attack (a DDos attack system). Rate limitation devices can be used on routers to halt requests when the volume becomes too great. Intrusion detection systems can detect the 'fingerprint' of the attack and alert upstream ISPs to put countermeasures in place[10]. The use of IP directed broadcasts is also a problem (utilised in Smurf attacks). Even if a site is not under attack, the facility should be turned off on routers[11]. However, these measures are not guaranteed to foil an attack. The biggest problem seems to be that, while a lot is known about hacker tools, they are changing quite rapidly. The side of innovation is always with the hackers. Elegant responses to attacks can be developed but, as the nature of the attack changes, the responses are not so effective. The very openness of the Internet is both its major asset and its major weakness[12]. Its capacity to promote technical innovation, which has been such a success, means it is also open to exploitation by those who have malice in mind.

6.2   Possible defence against attacks

Systems need to monitor whether they are being attacked. Intrusions need to be defined within the bounds of the individual system before they can be detected. A security policy should normally define what constitutes an intrusion. Intrusion definitions will obviously vary between systems, as each will have distinct security requirements. An intrusion can be defined as any set of actions that attempts to compromise the integrity, confidentiality, or availability of a resource[13].

There are two major classifications that can describe intrusions:

1. **Anomalous intrusions** are based on deviations from normal user behaviour.
2. **Misuse intrusions** exploit some vulnerability in the

system's hardware/software in order to achieve unau-thorised access.

A basic method to determine whether an organisation is being attacked is via the use of Intrusion Detection Systems (IDS).

Fundamental techniques

Many IDS follow techniques that monitor and analyse audit trails supplied by the operating system. These audit trails allow certain behaviours on the system to be identi-fied by keeping a record of such processes as hardware use and procedure executions. Therefore, the IDS can compare the behaviour of a system's users to individual profiles that represent their normal behaviour. Audit trails can also be used to detect known attack patterns. Audit trails are com-pared to a misuse signature that represents malicious behaviour; a match would infer an intrusion has occurred. Furthermore, statistics based on the activities of users of the system can be collected from audit trails to maintain and build up profiles to reflect user behaviour. Other IDS use state-based analysis to detect intrusions, for example virus checkers.

Audit-based detection

Intrusion Detection Systems require information on the behaviour of a system. Audit-based detection provides this information in the form of a series of operating system audits. The generation of audit records to form an audit trail for each user is the key aspect of audit-based IDS. Audit records provide information on the interactions between the user and the individual objects in the system. An audit record is generated for each interaction. Generally if more than one object is involved then separate records are produced. For example, if a file is to be copied then two records will be created – one that represents the reading of the file, another the writing of the file.

Audit records do pose some problems for intrusion detection due to the fact that the structure can vary across different platforms. There is no standardised format of an audit record; this means that the content of an audit record may have its own unique limitations and features. This creates a serious problem for intrusion detection systems in relation to their compatibility and adaptability. There have been attempts to standardise the information generated by audit trails, but this has met with little success. The generation of audit records to monitor system behaviour is an extremely small aspect of an IDS. These audit records must be somehow analysed. Special-purpose audit analysis programs that can adopt different approaches are used to analyse thousands of audit records per minute. This feature determines the effectiveness of the IDS. Some sophisticated systems have the ability to analyse, detect, and then respond to intrusions in real time.

Audit-based detection systems generally attempt to achieve at least one of the following:

1. Detect known attack patterns (misuse detection).

2. Detect deviations from normal behavioural patterns (anomaly detection).

3. Reduce large amounts of audit data to smaller amounts of meaningful information.

4. Filter audit data to provide summaries of trends.

5. Trend analysis.

However, there are complexities in misuse and anomalous detection that will be discussed in relation to IDS characterisation. Audit reduction (4) is a fundamental feature that all efficient audit-based IDS should strive to achieve. Audit reduction helps reduce the complexity of analysis. Trend analysis (5) is more associated with providing information for investigation but not necessarily detection. It allows some information to be analysed that would often be overlooked. Trend analysis could be effective in depicting a gradual attack on a system. For example, an attacker may perform quite a number of small attacks that on their own amount to little, but over time can form a substantial attack. Generally the most effective audit-based IDS would use a combination of these goals to improve performance.

State-based detection

State-based detection has been explored and is highly developed. However, it applies more to system-level detection. A good example of state-based detection is the virus checker. The number of known computer viruses today is around 30 000. However, this number will always be increasing. The virus defence community[14] identifies about five new viruses each day. Yet virus detection remains the most reliable intrusion detection technology, because of the continual development of virus detection software.

6.3 IDS characterisation

Intrusion Detection Systems (IDS) are characterised by focusing on two aspects – these are anomaly and misuse detection.

Anomaly detection

Anomaly detection makes observations of significant deviations from normal behaviour. A user profile describing normal behaviour can be used essentially to detect significant deviations in normal system states. This means that when a user's system behaviour differs from their 'normal profile', anomalous intrusions can be detected. However, there are problems associated with this detection method. There needs to be a balance between being too tightly and too loosely in line with the profile's 'normal behaviour'. The major approaches to anomaly detection:

♦ **Statistical:** behaviour profiles are generated for users. The system then constantly matches the profiles to user behaviour. These profiles are merged at certain time intervals. Statistical approaches learn the behaviour of users by updating profiles. However, this does reveal a problem – attacks can train the system so that an intrusion's behaviour will be considered normal (perhaps trend analysis, as described above, could minimise this potential for intrusion).

♦ **Predictive pattern generation:** future events are predicted by the knowledge of events that have already occurred. Therefore, if events A and B have occurred then there would perhaps be 85% chance that event C would occur next, or a 50% chance that D would be next. Patterns to predict user intrusion have benefits over statistical approaches as potential attackers cannot train the system.

♦ **Neural networks:** the neutral network is trained to predict the user's next command, based on previous commands. The network trains itself by recording user commands. It then compares actual commands to this profile thereafter. This approach, however, has a similar problem to the statistical approach – it can be trained.

Misuse detection

Misuse detection is based around representing known attack patterns in the form of coded signatures in order to compare, then perhaps generate matches with actual intrusive behaviour. Variations to these known attack patterns should also be able to be detected. The concern with this form of detection is that only the known attack patterns (and variations of it) can be detected. Therefore, new intrusive behaviour, unknown to the system, can slip past.

The major approaches to misuse detection are:

♦ **Expert systems:** this approach is based around rule matching. The expert system has the knowledge of known attack patterns. The database of encoded attack patterns can be modified depending on the platform it's operating on. The major disadvantage is that the expert system is created by a programmer, and therefore its effectiveness is very much determined by the programmer's ability to encode attack signatures.

♦ **Model-based intrusion detection:** this focuses on the idea that attack scenarios are comprised of certain activities that can be easily monitored. The approach uses an anticipator to predict the next action of an attacker, a planner to translate the attack scenarios into an audit data format, and an interpreter that searches audit trails for matches. The important factor with this approach is that attack scenarios need to be far from normal user behaviour.

♦ **Keystroke monitoring:** this approach monitors keystrokes for attack patterns. This technique is very simple and can be quite easily fooled by attackers. It does not have the ability to monitor applications, therefore intrusions such as Trojan Horses cannot be detected.

6.4   Defeating IDS

Research into IDS is not a highly developed area. There are many loopholes and techniques that can be employed to defeat less robust systems. According to Fred Cohn, a principal member of technical staff at Sandia National Laboratories, many of the commercial IDS products available to most businesses are 'poor at best'[15]. He proposed several methods that could possibly defeat some detection systems, some of which are:

♦ Insert extraneous characters into a standard attack command. For example, '&& true' will not effect the command but decrease IDS performance.

♦ Use tabs instead of spaces in commands. Most current systems do not interpret all separators in the same way. Also use ',' instead of ';' in a Unix shell.

♦ Change the separator character in the system. This would definitely confuse the IDS.

♦ Divide an attack across more than one user.

♦ Divide an attack across multiple sessions. Login once to begin the attack and then login again to complete it.

♦ Divide an attack across multiple remote IP addresses.

♦ Define a macro for a command used in an attack and use that instead of the actual command.

♦ Use different commands to do the same function.

♦ Encrypt attacks, for example by using the secure shell facilities, used to prevent snooping by attackers will also prevent snooping from the IDS.

♦ Add comments to a standard attack command.

♦ Type extremely slowly, over a period of a few hours per command. Buffer sizes are limited, therefore the attack traffic could be lost with everything else the IDS has to do.

♦ Kill the IDS by attacking the platform that it resides on.

♦ Generate false audit records. Create packets and send them in between attack behaviour.

♦ Use a translator program from commands.

♦ Start a session on an unusual IP port. These ports are often not understood or even watched by IDS.

♦ Attack over dial-ins instead of a network. This is a good tactic for network-based IDS.

♦ Create a large number of false positives. This will make the real attack difficult to follow up by human resources.

♦ Put the attack into a compiled program and get someone in the network to run it, for example a Trojan Horse.

A widely adopted method of breaking through firewalls is IP address spoofing. This works on the idea of masquerading as a host that is seen as 'friendly' to the system and is tolerated by the systems security. The problem that this can generate for some IDS is that, if a trusted host appears to have made the attack, it cannot be traced back to the real source.

IP address spoofing

To achieve IP spoofing there are several steps that must be followed:

1. The target host should be chosen.

2. A trusted host is discovered, along with trusted patterns of behaviour.

3. Disable the trusted host and the target's TCP numbers are sampled.

4. The trusted host is impersonated to make connection.

5. If successful, execute a command to leave a backdoor.

An ideal IDS would include a trusted host in its scope of detection using detection agents that could communicate across networks. Nevertheless, all IDS currently have a number of technical issues that reveal vulnerabilities. Such vulnerable features of IDS include:

♦ The balancing of false positives and false negatives. When more false positives are eliminated, more false negatives appear, and when more false negatives are eliminated, more false positives appear.

♦ There is minimal mathematical understanding of this field in relation to depicting known attack patterns and defining intrusions.

♦ There is no common database of attack patterns, unlike the virus detection field.

♦ Inconsistency of information from audit records over a variety of platforms. This reduces IDS portability and adaptability.

♦ Data sources are either too scarce throughout the system (allowing intrusions to sneak around the system) or are centralised (making the system vulnerable to attacks).

The fact that these issues are quite obvious to developers and indeed potential intruders leaves room for significant and extended research in the area of IDS.

Notes

[1] Dube, J. (2000) Reno Vows Action, in: *ABCNews*, 9 February 2000. URL: www.abcnews.com

[2] Glasner, J., McCullagh, D. (1999) Yahoo Outage Was an Attack? in: *Wired News*, 7 February 2000. URL: www.wired.com/news

[3] Richtel, M. (2000) Canada Arrests 15-Year-Old in Web Attack, in: *The New York Times on the Web*, 9 February 2000. URL: www.nyt.com

[4] Richtel, M., Robinson, S. (2000) More Major Web Sites are Targets of

Attacks, in: *The New York Times on the Web*, 9 February 2000. URL: www.nyt.com

5 Kovar, M. (2000) *$1.2 Billion Impact Seen as a result of Recent Attacks Launched by Internet Hackers*. Press release 10 February 2000. URL:http://www.yankeegroup.com

6 Reuters (2000) Ebay Claims No Lost Revenue From Hackers, in: *The New York Times on the Web*, 24 February 2000. URL: http://www.nyt.com

7 See URL: www.cert.org

8 Szucs, L. (1999) Distributed Attack, in: *ZDTV*, 8 December 1999. URL: www.zdnet.com

9 Devost, M. (2000) *Distributed Denial Of Service Attacks Raise Liability Questions*. 11 February 2000. URL: www.infowar.com

10 Brick, M., Max, K. (2000) In the Wake of Web-Site Hacking, No Easy Answers, or Solutions, in: *The New York Times on the Web*, 9 February 2000. URL: www.nyt.com

11 Cisco (1999) *Characterizing and Tracing Packet Floods using Cisco Routers*, 16 August 1999. URL: www.cisco.com

12 Markoff, J. (2000) The Strength of the Internet to be Its Weakness, in: *The New York Times on the Web*, 10 February 2000. URL: www.nyt.com

13 Longley, D., Shain, M. and Caelli, W. (1992) *Information Security – dictionary of concepts, standards and terms*, Stockton Press.

14 Tucker, A. (1997) *The Computer Science and Engineering Handbook*. CRC Press.

15 Price, K., Crosbie, M. (1999) *Intrusion Detection Pages*, COAST Laboratory, Purdue University.

7 | An I-War risk analysis model

7.1 Introduction

At the moment, extensive research is being undertaken by military and intelligence organisations in various countries on how to protect the military National Information Infrastructure (NII), but unfortunately little is being done to protect its economic aspects. Many companies are unaware of I-War and face enough problems trying to implement standard computer security countermeasures. This chapter offers a model that is being developed to try to help organisations determine the impact that I-War could have upon them and their organisations.

The risk analysis model has features considering the threats and vulnerability of the NII. The NII can be defined in the most simple terms as comprising those components that make up the national network within and over which information is stored, processed and transported[1]. Without the NII, there would be no electronic commerce, hence any damage to the NII would have a direct impact upon these services.

7.2 An overview of the I-War risk analysis model approach

The I-War Risk Analysis Model (IWRAM) is a system designed to be used by business organisations to help them protect against future risks to their computerised systems.

The system is based upon a risk analysis model (see figure 7.1).

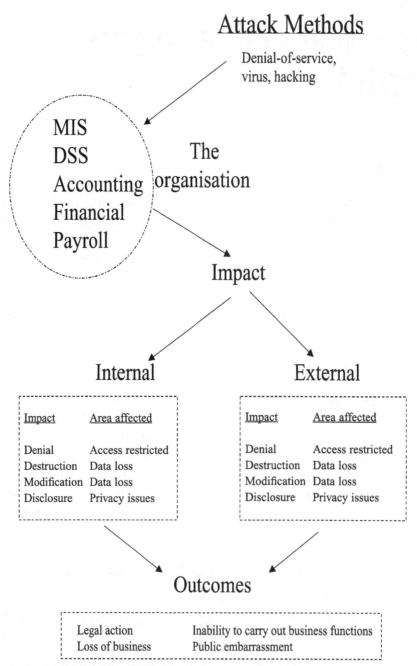

Figure 7.1: The IWRAM Model

The model is broken down into the following stages:

Stage 1: Attack methods

The user has to determine the appropriate attack method(s), which could be used against a particular organisation such as denial-of-service attacks, virus attacks, hacking, etc.

The attack can be focused upon a number of different aspects. For example, trying to crash the machine through denial-of-service attacks or trying to corrupt data through introducing computer viruses.

Stage 2: The organisation

After the attack methods have been selected in stage 1, the appropriate organisational computer system should be selected, for example financial systems or decision support systems.

The user has then to answer questions about the system, such as the importance of the data, how easy would it be to replace, what business function does the data support, etc.

Stage 3: The impact

The internal (the impact to the actual organisation) and external (the impact to customers/competitors/country) impacts should now be determined. This stage will show the impact that different attack methods could have upon an organisation. It helps to show the importance of the information contained on the organisation's computer systems and how they relate to core business functions.

The impact itself could be of various types – physical destruction of data, loss of business through lack of availability of system access, etc.

Stage 4: Outcomes and countermeasures

This stage suggests appropriate countermeasures to impacts determined in stage 3, for example recovery plans, mail filters, increased internet security, etc. This stage is concerned with reducing the impact that an attack could have upon an organisation.

This stage is complicated by the fact that countermeasures may have to be implemented at various levels to fulfil a particular security requirement, for example intrusion detection will have to be implemented at the server level, virus protection at the machine level.

Stage 5: Offensive countermeasures

This part of the model is concerned with suggesting offensive countermeasures which organisations can use. Most organisations have only defensive computer security countermeasures implemented. In the USA a new security approached called 'Strike Back' or 'cyber vigilantism'[2] has been developed. This is based on the use of offensive computer security features. The aim of this approach is to determine that an attack is occurring, and then automatically attack the attacker with the aim of stopping the unauthorised access attempt. This approach is not concerned with harming the attacker, but stopping an attack when it takes place before an organisation loses data or has it damaged.

This part of the model is the most radical since it can be defined as being unethical or illegal to carry out such attacks. But in the new millennium – new security paradigms may be more widely accepted to reduce security risks.

The IWRAM risk analysis model is different from conventional risk analysis models in the fact that it is event driven.

This new approach will result in a system that is more adaptable to organisational needs. This will help to make it proactive rather than reactive.

7.3 System design

It is important to develop a system that encapsulates the methodology. Therefore the following areas need to be looked at:

Environmental analysis

This analysis is concerned with determining the need for, and value of, knowledge within the organisations. Particular importance should be placed upon analysing the cultural environment of the organisations, for example staff interaction, management methods, etc.

User analysis

This is concerned with analysing the way in which organisations carry out their primary functions and determine their attitudes toward security issues. Another area examined is how organisations perceive the importance of their data. This will help them to become more aware of the data that has the greatest strategic value. This, in turn, helps to enhance their existing security, particularly for the data of the highest value.

Security knowledge

The security knowledge for the system can be acquired from a number of sources, including:

♦ relevant I-War literature;

♦ relevant I-War reports;

♦ results and analysis obtained from I-War questionnaires sent to major businesses;

♦ interviews with security and related experts;

♦ existing international/national security standards.

The knowledge reflected within the system contains the latest opinions and facts relating to I-War, but, as a matter of course, this information should be reviewed on a regular basis to ensure its current applicability.

The aim of the system is to produce a system which will give organisations an understanding of the impact caused by I-War. Another important feature of the system is that it suggests appropriate countermeasures.

7.4 Conclusion

This chapter has shown the importance of developing the IWRAM model and system. The event driven risk analysis model is a major departure from traditional risk analysis models and helps make systems more flexible in their approach to attacks.

It should also help raise awareness of the new I-War threat within the business sector, and make businesses consider more closely their place within the NII and take appropriate actions to secure that position.

Notes

[1] Defence Signals Directorate (1997) *The National Information Infrastructure: Threats and Vulnerabilities*, Government Publications, Australia.

[2] Hutchinson W., Warren, M.J. (1999) Attacking the Attackers: Attitudes of Australian IT Managers to Retaliation Against Hackers, *ACIS (Australasian Conference on Information Systems) 99*, Wellington, New Zealand. See appendix 4 for some more discussion on cyber vigilantism.

8 | Implications of I-War for information managers

8.1 Setting the scene

As an information manager[1] you grapple with the ever-increasing speed of software and hardware developments. Do the following describe your situation?

♦ Endless demands on your systems to keep the operational functions running (often at a 24/7 service level).

♦ Management has just demanded you produce an important report.

♦ Your programmers are leaving for better salaries.

♦ The quality auditors are knocking on the door.

♦ All three email server technicians are demanding holidays in the same month.

♦ The Help Desk clerk is crying.

♦ You are already late for your PowerPoint presentation to the Board.

In this environment, how can you consider the impacts and consequences of I-War to your organisation? It seems it has already broken out! The day-to-day survival we all have to endure in this accelerating world seems keeping the status quo a hard enough task to allow exotic concepts of I-War to impinge on our time. Leave it to security, they have nothing to do anyway!

Does this sound familiar?

Whilst many of us pay homage to such contemporary statements as the 'Information Age', the 'Knowledge Organisation', the value of critical data and so on, our behaviour is often very conventional. It has altered little from those secure mainframe days when getting into the computer room was as hard as getting out of Alcatraz, and terminals were really just simple versions of cable TVs. We gave the users the data they needed, and we determined what they needed. Security was relatively easy; very few people knew how to turn a terminal on, let alone hack into your systems.

However, we now live in a networked world, our systems are open, and the data distributed. There are a trillion people out there spending all day with the latest technology and every gismo invented just waiting to catch you out.

Senior executives **still** do not really understand the significance of the corporate database (in all its forms). They understand hackers; they have seen the movie! However, the concept of data/information/knowledge as a weapon or a target is only understood at a superficial level.

Very little can occur in an organisation until the critical nature of I-War is accepted. Its concepts need to be comprehended. They should be at the core of all organisational information strategies. The corporate database and its associated systems **are** the corporation. Information managers need embrace the concept of the organisation being a part of an internal and external matrix of people, machines, software, and data. In fact, today we are swamped with data. It is the responsibility of the information manager to facilitate the effective use of it. This means sifting out the inconsequential, verifying sources, protecting the significant (not spending millions to stop access to data that is of low value) and making sure it is **used** correctly.

How many organisations view their information managers as the corporate intelligence function? Very few. How many information managers view themselves as other than system administrators or data mining experts? In other words, they regard their main responsibilities as guarding data or ensuring it can be extracted when required. Of course, these are important aspects of the job, but in the long run, it is the acquisition of data, its interpretation, and its timely and effective use that are important. Once this emphasis is appreciated, the nature and priorities of the information manager's role change. It is necessary for mindset transformation to occur before this happens.

Both the appreciation and internal comprehension of I-War concepts are needed to develop the cognitive models necessary to change the organisational structures and activities required to survive in the virtual, networked world of today (not tomorrow).

If information (not data or knowledge) is power, then lack of it is weakness. The information manager must harness this power. The implications of this would seem to make the information function the most essential in the company. In a sense, it is the function that previously (in a slower world) was carried out by the board/CEO, or the managing director in a small company. The volume of data and the speed and complexity of social, economic, legal, political changes make this impossible now (although humans as sources of data and knowledge are still crucial).

It is the information manager's responsibility to facilitate the fighting of I-War. There needs to be redefinition of the information manager's place within the power structure of the organisation. It is essential that authority be placed where it is needed.

To understand the implications to information managers,

the three concepts of data, knowledge, and information will be used.

8.2 Organisational data

This is the realm of the conventional information manager. Over the years the nature of the data has changed from purely the operational, transaction-based data to data warehousing for strategic and futuristic enquiries. However, it is still the mindset of data storage which dominates. The dominant functions are to ensure the integrity, security, and timely availability of data. Whilst there may be some differentiation between types of data, most data is treated the same.

Internal data

Most organisations excel in the processing and storage of internal data. Systems are usually stable and their uses, by and large, accepted. However, there often is a need to understand the **value** of certain classes of data. This is often overlooked. It might be mentioned in a disaster recovery plan where certain systems are seen as crucial and need to be brought back immediately after failure. Nevertheless, the vulnerability to data loss/corruption, or its need to be kept confidential, is not so appreciated. The disaster recovery plan describes the operational vulnerability rather than the more tactical or strategic ones. The IWRAM model introduced in the previous chapter is a good starting point for managers to evaluate the exposure of the data under their care.

There is something deeper than this though. Conventional managers might understand I-War concepts from a security perspective, but baulk at the more proactive attack viewpoint. The skills needed for the intelligence function are not just looking after the data, but utilising it for organ-isational benefit, and in an aggressive way. This is not the traditional role of an information manager. However, until this is grasped, the organisation will not get the most out of its data, and information managers will remain computer-based boffins who are really the guardians of the technol-ogy. They really should be called technology managers. This is not a bad thing in itself, but does not exploit the potential of the data present in a company if that is the only 'information' function found.

External data

The acquisition of external data is much more problematic. The synergy between organisations and their clients'/sup-pliers' systems is increasing. This has been made available by such developments as the Internet and Enterprise Resource Planning (ERP) systems, which allow the free communication between the parties. However, these still are systems which only track data from the organisation's, relatively stable, immediate environment. The messier wider world of competitors, new technology, legal changes and so on are not so accurately monitored. It is this part of the intelligence function that needs to be looked at. Because this type of data changes quickly and is less predictable in nature, it is less suitable to the type of system with which we are familiar. It is more an art form than a science. This does not make it less important. It is essential to marry internal and external data to make effective management decisions. It is a function of the information manager to select, verify, filter, and distil external data using expertise found within the company. That is, a real **management** function, a real **information** function, and real **knowledge** function.

8.3 Organisational knowledge

Knowledge is really the province of individuals, although some would argue organisations could have knowledge which is more than the sum of its staff. How does an information manager harness this knowledge? A number of organisations have appointed knowledge managers, but often this means little more than another name for a function which already is the IT department. Sometimes they make the mistake of trying to document the full gambit of organisational knowledge. This misunderstanding of the concept and dynamic nature of knowledge leads to such innate things as recording a sales person's comments about a client. This subjective nonsense does not take into account the subjective nature of this data (because that is what it is, data), the active interaction between the personalities of the client and sales person, or the trivial nature of the 'knowledge' obtained.

The real benefit of using knowledge is in its dynamic nature. The 'expertise' found in an organisation should be harnessed, as it is required. The idea that it can be documented (as data is) is as fallacious as it is futile. Knowledge managers should be working with those in the organisation that can interpret data to produce useful information. If 'knowledge' can be brought down to an algorithm, then all well and good. The argument is that knowledge is a combination of algorithm, data and the ability to set the problem in context. By and large, software cannot do this; although in chapter 11 we will discuss perceptual intelligence software that does somewhat do this.

Knowledge managers need to ensure that the context and data presented to those making decisions have integrity. They should not have been corrupted or influenced by accident or design to the detriment of the organisation. The security function should also ensure that those with knowledge are making the decision with the best intentions toward the organisation rather than a personal agenda. This is important with internal employees as well as contract staff.

8.4 Information

The most important end product is information. This means information that has not been corrupted or detrimentally influenced. Rational management decisions can then be made for the benefit of the company. Ultimately, the information manager's supreme function is to make sure of this. All other functions are to make sure the production of information is made securely and in a timely fashion. The hardware, software, and staff are there to produce quality information. The objective of an 'enemy' is to ensure it does not take place. Attacks can be made on the hardware, software, personnel, or the external environment. The information function must make sure this does not happen.

8.5 Conclusion

When talking to the senior partner of a large regional law firm in England, a number of problems arose concerning their IT department. Although the company had developed a superb information system infrastructure **before** any specialised IT staff had been employed, the system was now stagnating. IT staff were treating users arrogantly, especially secretaries who had developed the systems in the first place. Innovations were taking up to a year to implement. Even getting a printer repaired was a nightmare. The IT department had forgotten why they were there. Their job was to facilitate information flow within the company. If you needed to fix a printer to do that, then all well and good. The point is that the emphasis was on

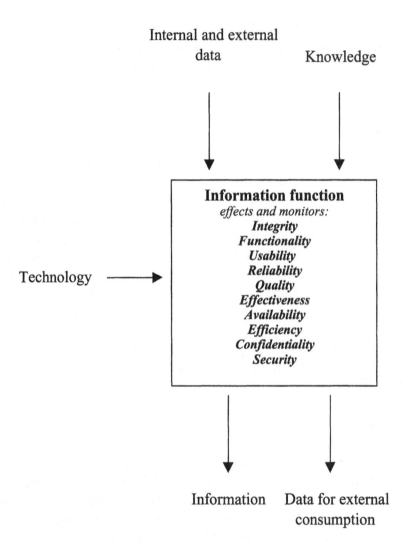

Figure 8.1: The information function

the technology, not the information that could be derived from it and the staff. The suggestion was made to change their name to 'Information Services'. This was done immediately; hopefully, it saved their jobs.

The point of this last tale is that the whole reason for having IT is to produce information. Obvious? Well yes, but not to many in the industry who seem to think that having a printer on-line is more important than having something to print on it.

Figure 8.1 (which makes a similar point made in chapter 2) summarises the point. The information manager's function should ensure that the technology, data, and knowledge within an organisation are integrated to produce information essential to the survival of that organisation. The technology is important but only as far as it facilitates the timeliness of effective information production. It is not an end in itself. The same could be said of data and knowledge. It is the **right** data and the **right** knowledge that are necessary. Once that obvious and simple fact is accepted then the protection and exploitation of them will take new forms. It is the implication of the word 'right' that needs to be thought about. Can we predict what will be 'right' tomorrow? Probably not completely, but that is really the task of every manager. Like all management activity there is never a one hundred per cent certainty of everything. The fun is getting close; that is the challenge for information managers. Figure 8.1 also shows the success factors needed to provide a secure and robust system.

Also illustrated in figure 8.1 are the success factors necessary to form the basis for a viable and successful system. Each of these factors needs to be addressed to adequately defend an attack in I-War.

Finally, the concept of an organisation exporting selected data is not normally lumped with the production of management information. Yet, it too is a part of the data/knowledge/information process. Often the realm of public relations or marketing, it is nevertheless very much a factor in I-War.

Note

[1] The term 'information manager' is used here as a generic to cover the whole gamut of roles and titles available such as information technology manager, computer services manager, knowledge manager, and so on. This chapter is really concerned with the function but, of course, humans with titles will carry them out.

9 | The legal perspective of I-War[1]

9.1 Introduction

A significant problem associated with I-War is that its governing legal principles are unclear. Questions remain largely unanswered. Where does I-War legally fit into the international and domestic environments, internal and external relations, state, corporate and business governance? When there is doubt and uncertainty, individuals, corporations and countries will inevitably seek to take advantage, to the detriment of others, of that doubt or uncertainty. If one accepts the reality that I-War is with us, both in the domestic and the international environments, and with us to stay, then the questions become:

♦ What laws currently exist that may provide all or any of the solutions?

♦ What can be done, especially by developing nations, to prevent or minimise the attendant risks?

Many existing areas of law could be relevant including international law, criminal law and telecommunications law and the significant areas must be briefly considered if proper responses are to be provided.

9.2 International law and I-War

There are currently no binding international agreements specifically dedicated to the control or prohibition of I-War nor are there any existing international agreements that even make specific mention of the term 'I-War'. Where then are we left within terms of international law and I-War? One must consider which existing international agreements could be interpreted in a way as to encompass or include within their provisions the term 'I-War'.

United Nations Charter

It is arguable that the United Nations Charter **could** apply to I-War if it can be construed that such warfare constitutes a 'threat or use of force against the territorial integrity or political independence of any state'[2]. Notwithstanding the fact that the Charter was drafted with armed conflict in mind, if one accepts that I-War is a form of aggression that attempts to force another country to undertake a particular action, then existing case law[3] would tend to support the view that I-War comes within the Charter.

Outer space treaties

Another significant body of law that **may** have an impact on I-War are the various treaties relating to outer space. Whilst outer space and cyber space may not be synonymous terms, they both know no territorial boundaries and if one accepts that I-War involves the use of communication systems in space then space law may well be applicable. There are a number of treaties that **could** be relevant[4] the most significant of which is probably 'The Treaty on Principles Governing the Activities of States in the Exploration and Use of Outer Space Including the Moon and Other Celestial Bodies 1967' (the Outer Space Treaty). The essential thrust of these treaties is that the use of space will be promoted for peaceful purposes. The fact that the treaties were not drafted with I-War in mind, coupled with the fact that the treaties were not confined only to peaceful purposes, becomes problematic. The treaties were drafted with 'weapons of mass destruction' in mind, and whilst no one would deny that I-War can have a devastating effect on the victim country, it is perhaps drawing a long bow to suggest that the global transfer of data and information via computing equipment is included in the words 'weapons of mass destruction'[5]. It is suggested that whilst I-War is not readily included, in the legal sense, within the words, it, in principle, should be so included.

It seems that if the satellite carries communications equipment that is an integral part of a larger system that actually causes or precipitates 'mass destruction' upon the enemy, then the satellite is indeed carrying a vital component of the weapon system as a whole.[6]

The problem with the treaties is that whilst you may be able to stretch or twist them to fit a particular case of I-War, they do not readily or easily fit and provide little, if any, real guidance, let alone enforcement ability.

Telecommunications treaties

Another area of international law that **may** well affect the issue of I-War is to be found in the Telecommunications Treaties[7]. When considered together, the broad thrust of the treaties is to ensure that non-military (namely civilian) satellites will be used for peaceful purposes 'so as not to cause harmful interference to the radio services or communications of other members'[8]. Accordingly almost all aspects of I-War would, on the face of it, fall within the ambit of the treaties for those states that are signatories to the treaties.

The Hague and Geneva Conventions

Another area of international law that must be briefly considered when dealing with I-War is the law of armed conflict as primarily codified in the Hague and Geneva Conventions. The thrust of these conventions is towards the protection of the civilian populations and to the defeat of the enemy forces with minimum necessary force. The words 'armed conflict' were designed for the geographical physical battleground and whilst some would argue that the underlying principles still apply to warfare waged in cyber space, it is suggested that, in practice, the conventions will be difficult to apply.

Customary laws

For the purposes of this chapter, the final area of international law that will be briefly considered is that of customary or traditional laws. Customary laws are the unwritten practices that have been consistently followed by the world's nations and which are enforced as mandatory laws through international institutions such as the United Nations. Where does I-War fit within customary law?

If the deliberate actions of one belligerent cause injury, death, damage, and destruction to the military forces, citizens, and property of the other belligerent, those actions are likely to be judged by applying traditional law of war principles.[9]

There is no certainty as to how the international community would apply or interpret customary laws in the case of computer network attacks. These are in largely uncharted waters. It is suggested that the international community will focus on the consequences of the I-War and not on the process or the mechanism by which it was effected.

Surely, no one is likely to dispute the fact that a victim country has been 'attacked' if the effect of the I-War was to close down the victim country's banking, air traffic control and financial systems. Given that there has been an 'attack' the nature of an approved and appropriate response becomes a vexed issue. An appropriate response, by way of defence, may well include a retaliatory computer network or traditional military attack. To gain international acceptance for positive countermeasure steps, there would need to be clear evidence (and that will not be easy to get) that the attack was attributable to the servants of the attacking country and may or may not require notice and opportunity being given to ceasing or preventing the offending conduct.

It seems beyond doubt that any unauthorised intrusion into a nation's computer systems would justify that nation at least in taking self-help actions to expel the intruder and to secure the system against re-entry. An unauthorised electronic intrusion into another nation's computer systems may very well end up being regarded as a violation of the victim's sovereignty. It may even be regarded as equivalent to a physical trespass into a nation's territory, but such issues have yet to be addressed in the international community ... If an unauthorised computer intrusion can be reliably characterised as international and it can be attributed to the agents of another nation, the victim nation will at least have the right to protest, probably with some confidence of obtaining a sympathetic hearing in the world community.[10]

Conclusions on international law

What is clear from the above discussion is that it will not be easy to apply existing international law to I-War. It should not be forgotten that the fundamental premise upon which international law is based is that independent states are legally equal and that the law, usually found in the form of bilateral or multilateral agreements or treaties, will only be binding in the manner and to the extent that each nation affirmatively agrees to be so bound. Only countries that are parties to the agreement will be bound by the agreement. The main reason that international law works is that signatory countries have 'voluntarily' agreed to comply with the terms of the agreements and to submit to the jurisdiction of the enforcement bodies[11] created pursuant to the agreements. Even if international law was to apply to a particular act of I-War, it is likely that in many cases the international law would not, in any event, legally apply to developing nations as non-signatories to any of the appropriate existing treaties.

9.3   National law and I-War

The focus of the discussion in the area of international law was largely upon the possibility of action being taken by one country against another country as a consequence of I-War. The problem with such a focus is that I-War may be perpetrated against a victim country by an individual, a small group of individuals, or a corporation acting alone (with no reference to or assistance from or connivance with the perpetrators' home government). Action by the victim country against the perpetrators' home country would not be a fair, reasonable nor an appropriate response. Further, in the business world, the impact of I-War upon a particular business (whether that business be a sole trader, a partnership, a large or a small corporation) can be as proportionately significant, and real to it, as an attack on a country's computer systems can be to that country. The interests of the corporate world have been, perhaps, a little lost or a bit forgotten in the area of I-War.

The actors in the international legal system are sovereign states. International legal obligations and international enforcement mechanisms generally do not apply to individual persons except where a nation enforces certain principles of international law through its domestic criminal law, or in a very limited class of serious offences (war crimes, genocide, crimes against humanity, and crimes against peace) that the nations have agreed may be tried and punished by international criminal tribunals.[12]

Brief mention must be made at this point of I-War and its impact in the commercial setting. It has been reported recently that in the past year one third of Australian businesses were the victims of some form of cyber attack (many, if not most, of which were from outside the organisation and not from a disgruntled employee). Yet only 40% of affected businesses reported the attack to relevant enforcement agencies[13]. Further, the incidents of attack had reportedly doubled in the last year[14]. The figures are likely to be more significant than reported when one considers the prevailing mentality of many corporations that it is unwise to admit that they have been the victims of an I-War attack because they felt that any such admissions will increase the possibility of further attacks. The response by government to I-War in the commercial world was, perhaps not unexpectedly, to consider the national interest and to leave it to the commercial players to fend for themselves. The government response was to indicate that it intended to investigate a framework to protect national information infrastructures including telecommunications banking and finance, transport, distribution, energy utilities, information services, defence and emergency services. By way of protecting the business sector, the suggestion has been made that all businesses be required, by legislation, to take affirmative steps to adequately protect themselves from the impact of I-War. Another suggestion is that all businesses be required to enter a form of compulsory insurance scheme. Another suggestion that has been made is that the scope, role, the funding of Computer Emergency Response Teams be expanded to facilitate greater protection from I-War to affected businesses. It is suggested that none of the suggestions are likely to be either effective or implemented in the near future. What is clear is that when one considers a response to I-War the inescapable bias will be directed toward the national interest and national security and the corporate world will only be a beneficiary of any actions taken to the extent that it falls within that interest.

If international laws are not readily going to apply in the above circumstances, what then will apply? The answer is to be generally found in the domestic law of each sovereign state.

The basis of national laws

Prosecutions for I-War-based actions within any nation are generally not possible unless there are domestic laws that specifically make the action in question illegal. Similarly, a country's enforcement agencies' power or authority to investigate I-War-based actions is dependent upon the actions being potentially or allegedly illegal. Most countries will have enacted domestic laws that in some way cover some forms of I-War. Perhaps the most common applicable body of law is to be found in the criminal law and there is a substantial body of national criminal law in place around the world concerning I-War and in particular computer crime and hacking. As an example, in the USA, federal laws provide for federal offences covering computer crime when computers are illegally used in interstate commerce or communications.

The very nature of domestic laws is problematic when one is considering a global and effective response to I-War. I-War is not constrained by national borders yet the jurisdiction or coverage of domestic laws is confined to the applicable sovereign geographical borders. Perhaps this would not be such a problem if circumstances were such that there were identical laws applying in all jurisdictions and there was complete co-operation between all the world's governments and all the world's enforcement agencies. But that is not the case! The reality is that the various applicable laws vary dramatically in their direc-

tion, their content and their sophistication and those variations are likely to continue at least into the immediate
future. The direction and content of domestic laws should
not be seen as merely a function of technological advance-
ment. It is also a question of attitude, opinion, and policy.
Some individuals, corporations, and countries would take
the view that the Internet (and all its interconnected computer systems) is a lawless and law-free zone and that it is
the right of all users to unrestricted and uncontrolled
access whatever the purpose. Clearly, some would like the
affluent and powerful to be 'put in their place' even if only
to a small extent.

Extradition agreements

Some would argue that extradition agreements might
provide a practical response to I-War issues. Such agreements may provide the answers in some cases but they
constitute a piecemeal non-global approach limited to the
countries that are parties to the agreement. Assistance and
co-operation between two countries' enforcement agencies
will generally only be possible if the alleged conduct is
illegal in both countries and, even if that is the case, a relevant and enforceable extradition treaty will also need to be
in place between the countries. If no such extradition treaty
is in place then the laws and penalties as applicable to the
alleged offence in the home country will come into play.

Extradition agreements generally oblige the parties to
deliver up the accused for criminal prosecution in the
requesting country but, of course, in the absence of such a
treaty, a country has neither the obligation nor legal right
or authority to deliver to the authorities of a foreign
country the accused for the purpose of facing prosecution
in that foreign country. Frequently, extradition treaties are
frustrated by limitations or exclusions to their operation,

and even if a treaty is in place it may not be effective in achieving its desired ends if it does not specifically cover, within its ambit, offences relating to I-War.

The way ahead with domestic laws

In the absence of a comprehensive international response to the legal issues surrounding I-War, it is imperative that each country brings its domestic laws up to a reasonable and comparable level as soon as possible. Given that I-War regards geographical boundaries as irrelevant, any weakness in the domestic laws of any one country may provide impunity to those who perpetrate I-War. Law enforcement in a country with effective and sophisticated laws covering I-War may well be impeded by a weak link in another country's laws.

It seems that there will be some international effort to resolve the incompatibility of criminal law at some point in the near future. Until such time, the best way for law enforcement to track hackers through diverse jurisdictions is through close co-ordination with investigators in the host countries and in strict compliance with their laws. This approach is not particularly rapid or efficient, but it respects the all-important concept of national sovereignty and causes no adverse international political ramification.[15]

9.4 The way ahead with international laws?

There have been some international efforts to respond legally to the issues raised by I-War. As early as 1995, draft treaty texts were to be found flowing around the Internet but to date no custom-built treaties are in place. It is suggested by the authors that there is little chance, at least in the immediate future, of there being a coherent international approach to dealing with I-War.

It is interesting to note that it has been reported recently[16] that unconfirmed reports circulating on the Usenet[17] suggest that the European Union, the USA, Canada, South Africa and other countries are currently drafting a cyber-crime treaty that, if implemented, would ban hacking and eavesdropping utilities. A translation from a note posted to the Politech mailing list states that the proposed treaty is to cover, amongst other things:

Protection against so-called CIA-crimes (confidentiality, integrity and availability) of public and closed networks and systems: computer hacking, unauthorised eavesdropping, unauthorised changing or destroying of data (either stored or in transport). In discussion are also denial of service attacks to public and private networks and systems ...

It is difficult to reconcile the above development with the US Department of Defense position stated in 1999 as being:

The United States has taken the position that it is premature at this point to discuss negotiating an international agreement on information warfare, and that the energies of the international community would be better spent on topics of immediate concern such as helping each other to secure information systems against criminals and terrorists.[18]

9.5   Conclusions on the legal perspective of I-War

The many legal issues surrounding I-War that deserve immediate and concerted attention of the international community and developing nations have a special role to play within the process.

Apart perhaps from action that can be clearly seen to be an attack on a country's vital infrastructures, the existing international and domestic laws do not leave one with any confidence that the legal principles adequately cover, or provide a proper response or enforcement mechanism to, acts of I-War. Unfortunately the likelihood is that the law will develop in a piecemeal fashion to critical situations as they develop from time to time.

In the immediate future, there is, at best, only a slim chance of a coherent and comprehensive international approach to the problem but undoubtedly such an approach is the required way forward. It will not be easy. Consensus will be difficult to achieve and it will be difficult to define the scope of any response. Given the relatively level playing field that exists between nations in the area of technology, the public announcements of developing nations as to their views, approaches and legislative direction in this area will have a real and meaningful impact or influence on the future development of international laws and/or compatible and comparable domestic laws.

There is a need for prudent planning and the co-operation of the international community. At a very minimum, there is a need for all countries to work together towards standardising domestic laws (in particular, criminal laws) and procedures.

As a matter of policy and strategy, and not law, there is the obvious need for nations to take affirmative steps to appropriately protect (through the use of appropriate technologies such as encryption and through the provision of proper training) their essential infrastructure, information and information systems. Of course, this is provided that in so doing there is no improper impact upon another nation's legitimate rights.

To conclude, a massive effort is needed to secure effective international consensus and harmonisation in the legal areas surrounding I-War. The response must have teeth. The laws, in whatever forms they take, must provide for effective enforcement mechanisms that are not confined by geographical boundaries. To avoid or minimise problems of state sovereignty or international law a clear legal basis for extended searches of computer systems and seizure must be established[19]. A global response is needed and deserved.[20]

Notes

[1] We are grateful and indebted to Mark Stoney of Edith Cowan University, Western Australia, for contributing the majority of this chapter.

[2] Article 2(4) of the Charter.

[3] United Kingdom v. Albania (1949) International Court of Justice (ICJ) 4; and Nicaragua v. United States (1986) ICJ 1.

[4] See the Moon Treaty – the Agreement Governing the Activities of States of the Moon and other Celestial Bodies 1979 and Liability Convention Treaty – the Convention on International Liability for Damage Caused by Space Objects 1973.

[5] Aldrich, R.W. (1996) *The International Legal Implications of I-War* (unpublished study, US Air Force Academy, Institute for National Security Studies, Colorado Springs, Colo., April 1996), 20.

[6] Di Censo, D.J. (1999) *Airpower Journal*, Maxwell AFB, 1999.
URL:http://proquest.umi.com/pqdweb?TS=943278@=
1&Dtp=1&Did=000000043514677&Mtd=1&Fmt=4

[7] International Telecommunications Satellite Organization Agreement 1973, Convention on the International Maritime Satellite Organization 1976 and International Telecommunications Convention of Malaga–Torremolinos, 1973.

[8] Article 35 of the Malaga–Torremolinos Convention, 1973.

[9] US Department of Defense (1999) *An Assessment of International Legal Issues in Information Operation*, May 1999 US Department of Defense – Office of General Counsel, p. 10.
URL: http://www.infowar.com/info_ops_061599a_j.shtml

[10] Ibid, p. 22.

[11] An example of an enforcement body would be the International Court of Justice.

[12] Ibid, p. 5.

13 From Bradford, S. (1999) *Courier Mail* (Brisbane, Australia), 16/6/99. URL: http://www.infowar.com/hacker/99/hack_061799c_j.shtml Similarly, 65% of companies polled in the UK in 1998 reported security breaches. The figures are likely to be greater than reported when one considers that.

14 See statistics Needham, K. (1999) Computer Emergency Response Team, *Sydney Morning Herald* (Sydney, Australia), 16/6/99.

15 Di Censo, D.J. (1999) *Airpower Journal*, Maxwell AFB, 1999, p. 8. URL:http://proquest.umi.com/pqdweb?TS=943278@= 1&Dtp=1&Did=000000043514677&Mtd=1&Fmt=4

16 To be found at http://www.infowar.com/law/00/law_012600e_j.shtml

17 To be found at http://www.http://www.bof.nl/cybercrime—treaty.pdf

18 Ibid, p. 50.

19 This was a recommendation (NOR (95)13) of the Committee of Ministers to Member States Concerning Problems of Criminal Procedure Connected with Information Technology, adopted by the Committee of Ministers on 11 September 1995 at the 543rd meeting of the Minister's Deputies, Council of Europe, Strasbourg, France.

20 This chapter was written early in 2000.

10 Political activists, freedom fighters, and terrorists on the Web

10.1 Introduction

It is difficult to determine the damage caused by politically motivated groups. The aim of this chapter is to try to determine the future impact that these organisations will have. The uses these political groups have made of the Web are analogous to more conventional organisations. No judgement is made about the aims of these terrorist/political groups. One person's freedom fighter is another's terrorist. Whatever your opinion of these organisations, it is interesting to observe how the power of electronic networks has been embraced by them.

As stated before, the growth of the Internet has led to a diversity of web sites. We are now facing a situation where terrorist/activist groups are developing internet sites and using network technologies. The areas where these groups are using the Internet are examined in the next sections.

10.2 Propaganda/publicity

Terrorist/activist groups have difficulty in relaying their political messages to the general public without being censored. The Internet has now provided a vehicle for this purpose. Some examples are:

♦ The Irish Republican Information Service[1] is a service

offering news articles (their interpretation) relating to the troubles in Northern Ireland. Sinn Fein[2] also offer their own site containing information about Sinn Fein, the armed struggle, policy documents, paper subscription, links to other sites, etc.

♦ The Zapatista Movement[3] have several sites detailing their struggle against the Mexican authorities. These sites offer information directly from the Zapatista movement, that is communiqués from the general command of the Zapatista Army of National Liberation. It is even possible to subscribe to electronic newsletters detailing the current status of the Zapatista movement.

♦ Third world terrorist/resistance groups have a cyber presence. The Tamil Tigers now have a voice through TamilNet[4] this includes general information, electronic newsletters and electronic magazines putting forward their points of view. Terrorist groups from Peru, the Philippines, Turkey, Columbia and the Middle East also have dedicated internet sites serving as propaganda tools.

It should also be stated that lesser known organisations are using the Internet to get their message across to a global audience. Examples include:

♦ East Timor Information[5]. This details the current human rights situation, their history, geography, culture and UN suggested resolutions about the territory.

♦ The National Council of the Resistance of Iran[6]. This details their political and military campaign against the Iranian government.

Some examples of web propaganda web pages can be found in exhibits 10.1 to 10.4.

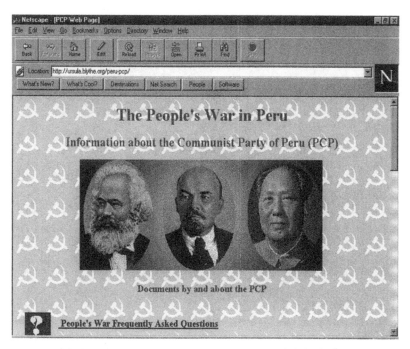

Exhibit 10.1: Communist Party of Peru's web site

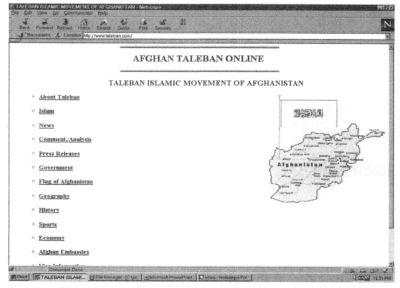

Exhibit 10.2: Web site of Afghan Taleban

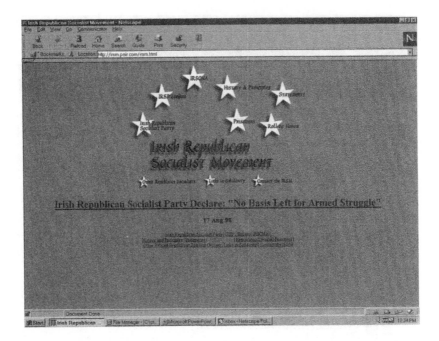

Exhibit 10.3: Web site for Irish Republican Socialist Movement

Exhibit 10.2 displays an interesting site – that of the Taleban. This group is opposed to modern technology yet they have a web site. The power of the message!

Almost as soon as the cease-fire was announced in Northern Ireland, the following Web page was put up (exhibit 10.4).

10.3 Fundraising

Some terrorist/resistance groups that are linked with political parties are now using the Internet for fund raising purposes. It is now possible to make direct donations using your credit card to Sinn Fein or via the use of mailing lists, to fund their political activities. In the future this may mean that the smaller terrorist/resistance groups may be

THE STRUGGLE
CONTINUES
WHILE ENGLAND REMAINS IN IRELAND
THERE WILL BE NO PEACE

It's Your Decision

Exhibit 10.4: Web site for 'The Real IRA'

able to receive the majority of their funding through credit card donations. These groups then will be able to fund their activities in a much more effective way. An example of a fundraising web site can be seen in exhibit 10.5.

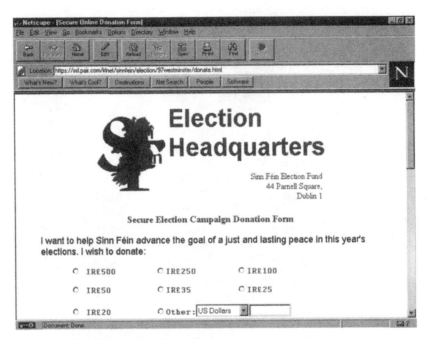

Exhibit 10.5: Sinn Fein fundraising web site

10.4 Information dissemination

It is now possible for terrorist/resistance groups to exchange information without being traced. It has been proven that paedophiles use the Internet to exchange illegal information[7]. It can be assumed that terrorist/resistance groups will also make greater use of the Internet, the extent to which is, at present, unclear.

Groups may publish sensitive information about a particular country. Sinn Fein supporters in the USA made public on the Internet details about British Army establishments within Northern Ireland[8] (see exhibit 10.6). Support groups can also be served with specific news of significance (see exhibit 10.7).

Exhibit 10.6: Web site giving information on British military forces

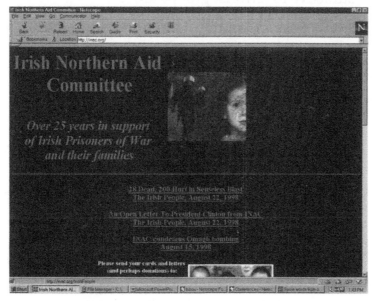

Exhibit 10.7: Support group web site

Information is available about engaging in terrorist activities. For example, *The Terrorist Handbook*[9] details the techniques for making explosives and weapons for beginners. The information contained within this document would assist any potential terrorists to develop their own bombing campaign.

It also is possible for terrorist/resistance group members on the Internet to have anonymous electronic remailers[10]. This shields their identity from public view. Once they have acquired an anonymous identity, any messages that are sent to this anonymous identity are rerouted to their email addresses. Individuals are also able to access email worldwide via the introduction of web-based email systems or by using mobile communication links.

10.5 Reasons why cyber terrorism will become widespread

Some reasons why cyber terrorism could become more attractive to terrorist groups are[11]:

♦ the risk of capture is reduced since attacks can occur remotely;

♦ it is possible to inflict grave financial damage without any loss to life;

♦ the expertise for these attacks can be hired;

♦ a successful attack would result in worldwide publicity and failure would go unnoticed;

♦ terrorist/resistance groups can attract supporters from all over the world;

♦ terrorist/resistance groups can use the Internet as a method of generating funds for their cause worldwide;

♦ the Internet offers the ideal propaganda tool for a terrorist/resistance group, one that operates on a global basis and that individual governments cannot control or censor.

So the advantages offered by cyber terrorist techniques mean that we are seeing many conventional terrorist/resistance groups develop internet strategies.

10.6 The development of cyber terrorist groups

Research[12] has shown that terrorist/resistance groups are now using the Internet for many different purposes, but these groups are now learning how to use the technologies of the Internet in order to advance their courses.

In order to describe this development of cyber terrorists, criteria have been developed which represent the levels of development for these groups. These levels are:

Level 0

The terrorist/resistance group does not use the Internet for any purpose and has just a physical presence.

Level 1

The terrorist/resistance group has a limited internet presence such as a web site and does not make use of other internet technologies. Their web site contains basic information about the group and their aims. Another category of level 1 is one in which the group has no official internet presence but their supporters have set up web sites on their behalf.

Level 2

The terrorist/resistance group has a moderate internet presence, and they make use of other internet technologies such as mailing lists. Their web site contains extensive information about political agenda, activities, etc.

Level 3

The terrorist/resistance groups have an extensive internet presence. Their web site is extensive. It contains more than just documents, including multimedia, sounds, images, etc. They have made extensive use of mailing lists and have set up a worldwide support framework of web sites amongst their supporters. These sites represent the support of these groups around the world.

Level 4

The same as level 3 but the groups are now carrying out limited information warfare attacks mainly hacking and rewriting web sites, denial-of-service attacks, etc.

Level 5

Information warfare is a major method of attacking the perceived enemy. Groups have an extensive worldwide support network and their web sites support the latest technologies and multimedia in order to get their message across.

Level 6

Groups at this level are of two kinds:

♦ The true cyber terrorist/resistance groups. These groups have no physical organisation and carry out no physical attacks. The group uses information warfare as its only attack method and attacks the perceived enemies' national information infrastructure and associated related computer systems. This group could also have a worldwide support base, and will operate and attack in the cyber world and not the real world.

♦ Physical terrorist organisations that carry out equal amounts of both physical and information warfare attacks. These groups use information warfare as an attack method and attack the perceived enemies' national information infrastructure and associated related computer systems as well as carrying out physical attacks.

What we have is a situation where terrorist/resistance groups are beginning to develop from one level to the next. An example of this is the Hezbollah group; their initial internet presence was focused on a web site that contains just limited information – level 1 (see exhibit 10.8). This web site simply represents a propaganda tool for them to get their message to the outside world without any political constraint or censorship.

The group developed their basic site into something much more advanced (see exhibit 10.9). It contains extensive information about their military campaigns and political activities. The site also contains extensive information about their operations from all around the world, not just their own resources, and includes readers' letters, where individuals can openly support the aims of Hezbollah, cartoons, various images, etc. and also email access to the organisation. They have now become a low level 3 group. They still have to develop the web-support network and mailing lists, but they do allow supporters to ask questions; these are put on-line to show that they have worldwide support.

The multimedia aspect of the site includes pictures taken of combat situations, video clips of news reports and audio recording of Hezbollah speeches.

The next logical development for Hezbollah internet plans is to expand their worldwide cyber support network. They

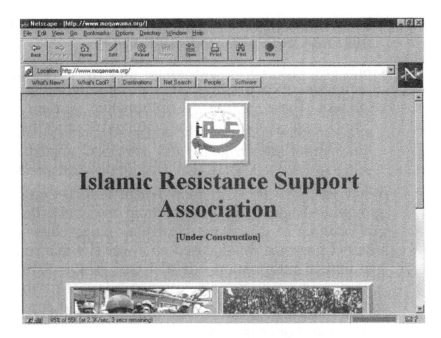

Exhibit 10.8: Old Hezbollah site

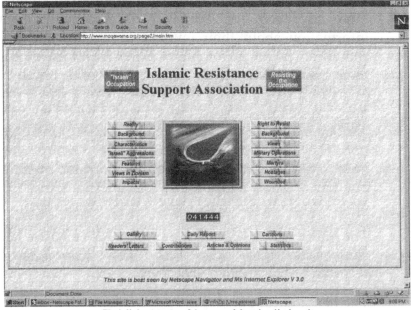

Exhibit 10.9: Newer Hezbollah site

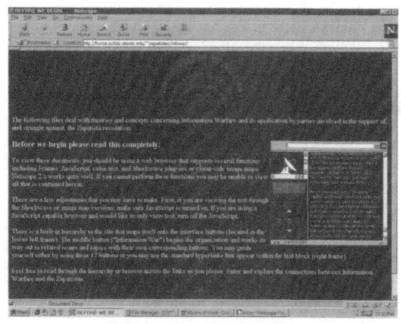

Exhibit 10.10: Zapatista site

Exhibit 10.11: Anti-McDonald's site

might also start to carry out simple information warfare attacks such as the hacking of web sites or carrying out denial-of-service attacks – in effect becoming a level 4 group.

10.7 Social activists

Not all political hacking is motivated by terrorist organisations, some are just motived by left or right wing political aspirations.

During the anti-World Trade Organisation riots in Seattle in 1999, not all the criminal activities were restricted to people throwing stones and bricks. The Seattle Host Organisation's web site, which sponsored the World Trade meeting, was the victim of denial-of-service attacks as well as numerous hacking attempts.

Some political activities are more general in nature. For example, anti-'Americanism' campaigns have spread to the Internet focusing on US businesses. An example, shown in exhibit 10.11, is the anti-McDonald's web site which purports to post 'the Truth' about McDonald's.

10.8 The future

It is difficult to predict how terrorists/resistance groups may use the Internet in the future. The previous table shows the diverse range of groups presently using the Internet. The following are areas of possible future internet usage:

♦ Internet attacks
Terrorists/resistance groups are starting to use 'hacking' as a means of attacking computer systems for political reasons, i.e. Zapatistas – Mexico (1998) (see exhibit 10.10), Portuguese Hackers – East Timor (1998). This

could result in entire computer systems being destroyed and would cause a dramatic impact upon related businesses and customers. It should also be remembered that knowledge of networks and computers will become more common in the future. Some groups have also carried out denial-of-service attacks, such as the Tamil Tigers' denial-of-service attack against Sri Lankan embassies[13].

◆ Improved electronic communications
More advanced encryption methods and improved anonymous electronic re-mailers will result in a command system that is difficult to break and allows for the command of terrorists/resistance groups anywhere in the world. This also means that attacks upon governments' interests can occur anywhere in the world, which will cause problems for the security services; it will mean that they will have to spend more time and resources on trying to decrypt electronic messages.

◆ Improved propaganda/publicity
The Internet will allow terrorist/resistance groups to get their uncensored messages to a global audience. This may increase their funds and also their support base across the globe.

10.9 Response to the problem

The seriousness with which the issue of cyber terrorism and information warfare is taken can be illustrated by recent activities by national governments. In the USA, for example, concern over IT related threats has led to the establishment of the National Infrastructure Protection Centre (NIPC). This is a $64 million facility, employing some 500 staff across the country, with representatives taken from existing agencies such as the Secret Service, the CIA, NASA, the National Security Agency, the Department of Defense and several others. The role of NIPC is to 'detect, deter, assess, warn of, respond to, and investigate computer intrusions and unlawful acts' that threaten or target US critical infrastructures such as telecommunications, energy, banking and finance, water systems, government operations and emergency services[14].

Whilst the threats are undoubtedly serious, we must be careful to ensure that the methods of response are not taken too far. Without appropriate control, it is possible that measures could be introduced that are harmful to society in a different way. For example, the complete regulation or monitoring of our use of IT systems could lead to the emergence (some would say extension) of a 'surveillance society' in which technology is used to erode individual rights and freedoms in the name of the wider public good[15].

It can already be seen that the activities of both hackers and cyber terrorists ultimately have the effect of restricting freedoms for the rest of us. For example, despite some concessions, the USA continues to maintain a relatively restrictive policy on the use of cryptographic technologies. One of the stated reasons for control is to prevent unregulated use of strong encryption techniques by terrorist organisations[16].

10.10 Conclusion

It is possible to protect a single target against physical attacks, but when these targets become computer networks, and the attack method is via the Internet and may originate on the other side of the world, it becomes much more difficult.

It is now becoming more widely accepted that groups have the ability to attack targets using cyber terrorist techniques. Within the last two years, there has been continued development of cyber terrorist capabilities. What will these groups be able to do within a decade? Could the first true level 6 cyber terrorist organisation emerge?

Notes

1 RIS (1999) Irish Republican Information Services.
   URL: http://joyce.iol.ie/~saoirse/
2 Sinn Fein (1999) URL: http://sinnfein.ie/index.html/
3 Zapatista Movement (1999): URL: http://www.ezln.org/
4 Tamil Net (1999) URL: http://www.sn.no/~cyrinus
5 ETIS (1999) East Timor Information Site.
   URL: http://www.uc.pt/Timor/TimorNet.html
6 NCPI and NLAI (1999) National Council of Resistance of Iran & National Liberation Army of Iran.
   URL: http://www.iran-e-azad.org/english/nla.html
7 *The Times* (1996) 13th November, UK.
8 *The Times* (1996b) 26th March, UK.
9 Anon. (1994) *The Terrorists Handbook*, USA.
10 Malik, I. (1996) *Computer Hacking: detection and protection*, Sigma Press, UK.
11 Warren, M. (1997) *The Use of the Internet by Terrorists and its Impact upon Business*, InfoWarcon 97, Brussels, Belgium.
12 Warren, M. (1998) *Cyber Terrorism*, SEC-98-IFIP World Congress, Budapest, Hungary.
13 Associated Press (1998) *First cyber terrorist action reported*, 6th May, USA.
14 NIPC (1999) Mission Statement, National Infrastructure Protection Centre. URL: http://www.nipc.gov/
15 Davies, S. (1996). *Big Brother – Britain's web of surveillance and the new technological order*, Pan Books Ltd, London, UK.
16 FBI. (1998) *Encryption: Impact on Law Enforcement. Information Resources Division*, Federal Bureau of Investigation, Virginia, US, 8 July 1998.

11 Perceptual intelligence and I-War

11.1 The 'personalised' computer

The previous chapters have been primarily concerned with the impacts of I-War on organisations. This chapter covers the more personalised developments in IT. The basic components of this new technology are:

♦ Wearable and portable computing power.

♦ Wireless technology.

♦ Perceptual hardware and software.

♦ Perceptive hardware and software.

The first two factors enable computer power to be carried by individuals, and obtain, as well as send, in real time mode. Hence, the mobile individual or device can communicate and react to instructions from a central point or between numerous other nodes in the network. Of course, this still implies some form of organisation. The opportunities to disrupt or corrupt this type of system are very similar to the tactics alluded to in the previous chapters. However, new technological developments are not only making data processing mobile, they are actually changing the nature of how data is presented and received. These new concepts actually try to extend the senses of individuals to make a truly computer-based functioning human. Leaving aside the desirability of this trend, the technology is already with us. We will only consider individuals in this context here, but networked versions of these devices are just as possible. These latter systems evoke monstrous 'Big Brother' scenarios when combined with the more personalised technology presented below.

11.2 Perceptual systems[1]

Contemporary systems tend to use a very limited set of human senses for output interpretation (for example, vision and hearing) and human actions for input (for example, movement on a keyboard, or voice). The development of perceptual systems and wearable devices enables a myriad of human senses to be used as output, such as pressure, sound, smells, chemicals, and taste. These systems become a part of the senses of the humans using them. Corrupting signals in these systems can thus have a profound effect on the users' perceptions of the world.

11.3 Perceptive systems

The real revolution comes from the type of input device that can be integrated into these systems. The point of these devices is not just to improve the existing senses but to add to them. Hence, devices which give extended telescopic vision might be supplemented by infrared vision. Sounds can be amplified with various devices, but others can detect normally inaudible frequencies and allow them to be displayed in a way which reinforces the user's perception of the world. However, although these devices enhance the user's perception of the world, they are not perceptive. It is the human who is perceptive.

Perceptive systems actually make decisions about the world without human control. Hence, they proactively search for data and filter it from the environment to feed back to the human or just act without any human interaction. For instance, an 'intelligent suit' might change colour depending on the environment it was in, or heat or cool depending on the temperature. A navigation system might report back when it has calculated that the travelling time to a destination is such that there is a likelihood of being late. It could detect chemicals in the air to indicate a gas spill, the presence of a human, or a restaurant! It could be monitoring your bodily functions and reporting back to the medical services your position and state of health. The applications are endless.

The personalised human/computer system would thus extend senses and enable interaction by the movement of a limb, a whisper in a microphone, the blink of an eye, or the nod of a head. Feedback data could come from a whisper in the ear (for example, 'someone is behind you'), a pressure on the neck, a flash to your eye, or a smell.

The point of these systems is that they are constantly providing feedback to augment your own. It does not take much imagination to envisage the kind of reliance individuals would place on them. Face recognition systems could remind you of a person's name and save that all too often embarrassment. Itineraries could be spelt out every morning with the appropriate travel details.

The kind of reliance placed upon these systems and their intimate nature make them prime targets for personalised I-War. Of course, if they were networked, the potential for altering perceptions *en masse* would be enormous. The principles outlined in chapter 1 would still be relevant as is the model presented in figure 1.3.

11.4 I-War against the individual

Perceptual/perceptive systems give almost perfect vehicles to execute I-War against individuals. These systems go straight to the senses of the human and, as such, enable the attacker to manipulate 'reality'. Hence, the nightmare of systems of networked individuals whose interaction with the real world came almost entirely through the artificial system.

The nature of perceptive systems enables the attacker to manipulate the environment to 'fool' the receptors into 'believing' that an action should be taken when it need not be. For example, the release of chemicals could emulate an event. Much like fooling an individual's senses, the manipulation of the environment could fool the technology. Certainly, 'dazzling' (explained in section 3.2) is a tactic that comes to mind. Overloading the systems with stimuli could confound it for a time. Depending on the reliance of the human on the system, this could provide a distraction at the very least.

Intuitively, the best part of the system to attack would be the sensors (and indirectly) recorders (see section 1.4); in other words, input and output devices. Camouflage or other deliberately erroneous signals could fool sensors. Of course, this would result in corrupted output on recorders. The whole point of this would be to produce an effect in the human receiver (or maybe, non-human activator). A change of behaviour is required and this would seem the easiest way to achieve this. All the other methods can be used, but unless the system is on-line they would be more difficult. Having said that, electromagnetic or radio devices could certainly disrupt them.

It is an interesting point of discussion that, as we become more reliant on IT in our organisational life, the development of I-War is also progressing. Will this also occur if as individuals we also become ever more reliant on these extensions of ourselves?

Note

[1] A very useful reference document for this technology can be found in *Communications of the ACM*, **43**, 3. This is the March 2000 edition and contains very readable articles on Perceptual Intelligence, Multimodal Interfaces, Haptic Interfaces, Visual Intelligence, and so on.

12 | The future

We live in a world where the US government treats strong encryption as a weapon because of its potential use by terrorists and criminals (and ordinary citizens?) to remain anonymous, where the British government sets up a centre to monitor all email traffic, and the Australian government openly gives its intelligence service the right to monitor and **alter** data in the interests of national security. This latter example must call into question the integrity of any electronic data, especially when used in court. Also, in this environment, the concept of completely confidential data is meaningless. Just to make sure this is the situation, the British government has now made it compulsory for persons to divulge to law enforcement agencies any encryption key when asked. The persons so asked must not divulge the fact that they have even been asked to do this. One can only speculate on the conflicts of personal and corporate loyalties this will create.

The irony is that as more and more data becomes available, the more it is monitored. Of course, this occurs at the national level with software scanning for keywords on telephone and computer systems; thus flagging the message, the sender, and the receiver for possible closer examination. At the corporate level, all emails are recorded (if not examined), and all internet searches logged. Censorship can occur by software disallowing certain web sites or email addresses. Hence, not only are your entire intimate electronic messages available to those with the power of access, but they are logged and remain a history of you as long as they are kept (this can be for a long time for corporate legal reasons). This coupled with more intrusive surveillance technologies such as cameras and listening devices must alter relationships between staff in a company. Can management and individuals always be relied on to act with integrity? The ability to corrupt the data produced is enormous. In fact, the potential to cause organisational disruption must be a mighty temptation to any adversary.

As more of the human environment becomes completely or partially under the control of computer systems, so will the human computer interface develop. For instance, future soldiers will wear computer systems on their bodies. These will add to human senses and give the warrior the ability to see in the dark; target, fire and forget; determine position to a couple of metres; communicate with commanders; send readings, images, samples; monitor for biological or chemical weapons; monitor body functions to provide real time medical data and advice; provide some electronic invisibility; and many other functions. This technology will have spin-offs in the civilian realm. Research is already taking place into wearable computers and peripherals for civilian use. Data will be viewed through special eye-glasses. Emails, visual, and auditory messages will be received on the move. Hyperlinks can be made dynami-cally. For example, walking the street an individual might see a street sign, and remotely link to a street map. Friends could be contacted to show them what the user is seeing via your portable digital camera. The applications become infinite. The recent phenomenon of mobile telephones, and the reliance some put on their possession and use, will indicate the dependence these mobile computers will create. One can envisage a suit which monitors the medical condition of the wearer, and registers any collapse. An automatic distress call can then be made, and the patient's locality and medical history relayed to the ambulance sent to deal with the situation. The same system could be used to alert the police of a robbery attempt, etc. Who could do without this? It also creates the possibility to create enormous disruption using these systems. Also, individuals could be constantly monitored (as some company vehicles already are), their life history could be continually logged: the people they meet, their reactions to them, their locality, what they spend, and so on.

Computer developments in terms of processing and accessing speeds will allow computers to crack encrypted messages a lot faster, as will 'quantum' computers if their potential is realised. In fact, these latter computers will make present encryption techniques redundant. The further development of security and offensive I-War software will be able to take advantage of the increased potential of this hardware.

The development of nano-technology will also increase the development of miniaturised cameras and other devices for spying. It has been postulated that a nano-machine can be created to fly around offices undetected collecting and transmitting visual, chemical, and sound data. Many less mobile nano-machines can also be created to collect and transmit specific data and remain undetected. Of course, techniques to counteract these 'bugs' will be developed. Their I-War principles will remain the same, that is, destroy the 'bugs' or their ability to function, or feed them the data you want them to pick up.

The progression of biotechnology also has implications for I-War. Bacteria or fungi can be developed to destroy computer equipment. A true computer virus! (Apologies to any biologists, we realise that our classification skills are a bit awry.) Also, the progress of the human genome project has enormous implications for individuals. Genetic data related to individuals would be of interest to such agencies as health insurance companies and potential employers. It would be of great value to an adversary. In fact, the vulnerability of medical data in general is not universally recognised. The ability to cause harm by altering individual or group records is vast. They can often be the source of much material, which can be used to blackmail. Knowledge of genetic make-up can expose susceptibility to physical or psychological illnesses. Medical records can expose actual illnesses and events. The point will not be laboured but those with harmful intent do not need much imagination to develop successful strategies. As a corollary to this, there is a proposal in Britain to store birth to death medical details of individuals electronically. Whilst this has some obvious advantages, it does not take a lot of deep thought to list many dangers and potential problems for privacy, potential abuse, and successful operation and maintenance. Is this another case of a superficially good idea leading to another expensive disaster?

The progress of the art/science of computer forensics techniques will aid in information defence by allowing for the apparent verification of such things as file integrity, date of production, and the source of a message. However, the study of these techniques will also be of benefit to an attacker if they are used to fool any investigator into believing that a file is valid, or that a message was sent from a particular source. Like much in I-War, it is a double-edged sword.

As our society becomes reliant on computers for its information systems, the concepts of I-War will become even more relevant. Paradoxically, the more we need to trust the data and its non-abusive use on our systems, the less we can. In the electronic world, it can be truly said that 'nothing is real', or will this new virtual world become the new reality? Anyone who has been a victim of identity theft (where such things as credit card details are used to order goods, or other acts are carried out in your name) might think this is the brave new world as they futilely try to prove their innocence.

The development of 'information weapons' has also made hardware system components vulnerable. Electronic systems are prone to damage by HERF (High Energy Radio Frequency) and EMP (Electro-magnetic Pulse) weapons[1]. One can only speculate the consequences of the ownership of these weapons by criminal and terrorist groups.

As I was writing the last lines of this chapter, a news item came over the BBC World Service. The head of France's counter-intelligence organisation is opening a judicial investigation into the USA's use of the worldwide ECHELON surveillance system to obtain economic data to the detriment of France. Ironic really, as the Americans constantly claim that France uses its intelligence service for economic espionage. The British and Americans claim that it is a French move to split the US/UK alliance ... the game goes on!

Note

[1] See Schwartau, W. (1994) *Information Warfare* – second edition, Thunder's Mouth Press, New York, and Sample, I. (2000) 'Just a Normal Town,' in: *New Scientist*, 1 July 2000 for discussions on these weapons.

Appendix 1 | Checklist for an information attack

The concepts introduced in chapter 1 can provide a framework for developing a successful information attack. Below is presented a number of questions to aid in formulating strategies and tactics.

What is the aim of the attack, and the desired end result?

Foremost in any attack planning must be the reason for carrying it out. Is the attack a part of a general strategy to achieve information dominance? Is it a specific attack to achieve a much more limited goal?

If the attack is part of a more general strategy, the other aspects must be co-ordinated. Who is responsible for this co-ordination? Are the timings of consequences and events relatively predictable or problematic? What are the contingency plans, and who will develop these as the campaign progresses?

It is most important to know not only the reasoning behind the attack but also the desired end result. In other words, it can be reasonable to desire information dominance as an aim, but how will you know this has been achieved? What do you want to happen, and how will you measure your success?

How are you going to ensure the desired result?

Using the desired end result as a benchmark, how will you best get there? What are the alternatives? What is the greatest vulnerability the target has? Can the end result be obtained at all? Has the target got too much strength in the areas to be attacked? In other words, are the end results attainable?

What are the undesired consequences of these end results for the attacker? Will you be found out? If you are, what will be the likely outcomes? What reprisals are likely? Is the attack ethically and legally sound from your perspective?

What will be the item(s) of attack?

Is it data that needs to be directly attacked to produce false input to the information making process? Is it the context of the data interpretation that needs to be manipulated? If so, who are the targets? What individuals or groups need to be selected?

How will the attack be achieved?

If data is being attacked, is it desirable to manipulate or destroy it? Should the aim be to deny data to the 'enemy'? Should it be to obtain confidential, sensitive, or private data? How would you then use this? Would it be given to others to the detriment of the target, or to justify your actions?

Is it better to subvert the target's system by installing a logic weapon which will produce corrupted data?

If the target is the perception of a group of people, what is the best medium? Should you use the public media, selected individuals to spread rumour, or more specific and controllable avenues? What is the perception management plan? What is the time frame – long or short?

What follow-up measures need to occur?

If the campaign is successful, what follow-up measures are needed? Has the campaign opened up new opportunities?

If it has been unsuccessful, what remedial measures need to be taken?

Table A1.1 gives the framework for attack planning in tabular form. The three main items are:

♦ **Elements of the target's system**: this lists the main parts of an information system as developed in chapter 1. Part of the attack strategy should be to pick the parts of the system most likely to be vulnerable and to achieve the desired result.

♦ **Method to be used**: this lists the items to be attacked (data or knowledge) and the basic method of attack. For example, is data to be destroyed, manipulated, or is the context of the problem to be targeted.

♦ **Desired end result**: for each individual part of the attack the desired result should be determined, as should its relationship to other elements of the attack.

The other elements incorporated into any document with this table should be:

♦ **Overall aim of the attack.**

♦ **Overall desired end result.**

♦ **Legal implications.**

♦ **Possible negative effects and contingencies.**

♦ **People's roles and responsibilities.**

Table A1.1: Table for planning an information attack

ELEMENT OF TARGET'S SYSTEM		METHODS TO BE USED						DESIRED END RESULT
		Data			Knowledge			
		Deny	Disrupt	Destroy	Change	Steal	Perception	Context	
SENSOR	Active								
	Passive								
OBJECT/EVENT									
PROCESSORS									
CONTAINERS									
RECORDERS									
CONTEXT									
HUMAN RECEIVER									
NETWORKS									

Appendix 2 | Using the Viable System Model as a framework for an information attack

The Viable System Model (VSM), developed by Stafford Beer[1] using the principles of cybernetics, has been successfully used to diagnose existing organisational structures and design new ones. As Espejo[2] states 'VSM provides a language in which to appreciate the complexity of organisational tasks and the communication mechanisms underlying people's interactions'. It is the generic nature of the VSM that allows it to be used in a myriad of circumstances for organisational analysis. It is a metaphor for a robust organisation (system), and can be used to analyse organisational health and other systemic problems. However, its insights into the requirements of maintaining a viable organisation can also provide clues to the mechanisms for destroying the same. This section will use this model as a framework to analyse potential vulnerabilities to an organisation's information systems. Its ability to be used in this manner demonstrates VSM's insights into the requirements of a functioning system.

Before using the VSM, it is essential to understand the dynamics of its applicability. The VSM consists of five sub-systems, which have the following functions:

1. **Implementation/Operations** (S1): this function consists

of semi-autonomous units, which carry out the operational tasks in the system. These are the functions that are basic to the existence/purpose(s) of the system. They interact with their local environment, and each other. Each unit has its own local management, which is connected to wider management by vertical information flows. This function is the 'doing' part of an organisation. The VSM has a recursive element, and each S1 has another VSM embedded in it.

2. **Co-ordination** (S2): this function co-ordinates the S1 units to ensure that each S1 unit acts in the best interests of the whole system, rather than its own. This could be represented by something as simple as a timetable, or as subtle as morale among the workforce.

3. **Internal Control** (S3): this function interprets policy information from 'higher' functions (S4), and 'lower' functions. It is the function which controls the operational levels. Its function is not to create policy, but to implement it.
Information arriving from the S1 function must periodically be audited for its quality and correctness. This is the S3* audit function.

4. **Intelligence and Development** (S4): this function acts as a filter of information from the S3 function and the overall outside environment. Its purpose is to ensure that the policymaking function (S5) is adequately briefed, and decisions are transmitted to S3.

5. **Strategy and Policy** (S5): this function is responsible for the direction of the whole system. It must balance internal and external factors.

Beer contends that all the above functions must be adequately performed in an organisation to keep it viable. It should again be noted that the model has a recursive element. Each S1 unit has embedded in it another VSM. Hence, the local environment now becomes the total environment for that system, and so on.

The VSM concentrates on functions but provides an effective tool for specifying information flows throughout the organisation. It explicitly states what needs to 'go on' in a healthy system, and hence the information channels needed to ensure this. It illustrates the need for both internal information for stability, and external information for survival in its environment. The comprehensive nature of the model enables it to be used to design information system strategies, and examine any missing components. Obviously, these qualities can be used to build and expose weaknesses in existing systems. However, these same characteristics can be used to attack organisations, and exploit weaknesses.

Attacking the organisation

A planned attack can be made at the operational, tactical, or strategic level. Roughly, these three levels can be mapped against the S1, S2/S3, and S4/S5 functions of the VSM respectively. Also, they can be equated with the efficiency, effectiveness, and vision/purpose of the organisation. Another perspective can be based on time. In this case, the objectives may be short, medium, or long term. In a world of a ubiquitous mass media, and instant, universal communications 'the distinctions between the tactical, operational, and strategic tend to blur into insignificance'[3]. For example, a campaign of misinformation claiming food poisoning caused by a particular product picked up by the mass media can change a local affair to a strategic one as the producer's total environment becomes involved.

Each specific function will now be examined. However, the

recursive nature of the VSM, with each S1 having VSM embedded in it, should be noted.

Attacking the fundamental operating units (S1)

The operating units can be disrupted by:

♦ **denying** them their operating (local) environments;

♦ **disconnecting** them from other S1 units;

♦ **separating** them from the management functions.

Information can be used to misinform both the local environment and the S1 units. This can cause a decrease in the beneficial relationship between the two. Disrupting the relationships between S1 units can result in the fragmentation of the whole operations function. This can be achieved by giving different information to each S1 either internally, or from the environment. This will cause a misreading by S1 management units of both their own local environments, and the performance of other S1 units. Attacks on the information flows from S2 and S3 can lower the effectiveness of S1 management.

Attacks on the S1 units are intended to decrease the efficiency of the whole organisation by disrupting its operational (production) functions. It can be viewed as analogous to the classic, military aim of 'breaking the line'. Here the attacker's objective is to disperse the enemy by such things as a concentrated attack on a specific part of the line, or striking at its flanks. In information warfare terms, this means using information tactics to cause chaos to a specified S1 unit (a direct attack), or disrupting the information between S1s and/or higher S2/S3 functions (a flanking move).

Attacking the co-ordinating function (S2)

The purpose of attacking the co-ordinating function (S2) is to destroy the cohesion of the operating units. Such simple things as a timetable, production schedule, or more abstract entities such as staff morale can bring about cohesion. Therefore, the aim of the attacker is to manipulate, change, or deny information to make this co-ordinating function ineffective. Thus, the activities of S1 units would be unco-ordinated at the very least, and working against one another to the point of complete disruption in a highly successful attack. An example might be to spread misinformation designed to create negative perceptions amongst staff thereby causing a loss of morale.

The co-ordinating function can be disrupted by direct attacks on communication or information systems causing the malfunction, or more indirectly by subtly changing pertinent information causing the integrated functions of the S1 units to fail. Classic psychological operations can be used against the victim's staff (as it can be in the local S1 environment, and more general organisational environment to change perceptions of customers, suppliers, authorities, and the public).

Attacking the controlling function (S3)

The main point of attacking the control function is to use information to disrupt the interpretation of policy. Thus, the instructions passed down to the S1 units would not be commensurate with the intentions of the policies created by S5. Altering information coming into S3 from S1 and S3*, and leaving S3 for S4 will also disrupt or misinform S4. Hence, the formulation of policy will be corrupted by 'bad' information, or be less effective because of lack of information.

Attacking the S3 function should disrupt or destroy effective co-operation between the planning/policy aspects of the organisation and its operating functions. The main intention is therefore to make the operational units either non-functional, or to function in a way that is at odds with the policymaking function, and to the benefit of the attacker. Therefore the destruction, or probably more effectively, the corruption of information going in and out of the S3 function is the attacker's aim.

Destroying the 'brains' and 'senses' of an organisation (S4/S5)

The purpose of the S4 level is to be the interface between the external and internal environments by processing and communicating information to S5 and S3. S5 produces policy from the information sent by S4. These two functions can therefore be seen as the 'brains' and 'senses' of the organisation. Therefore, the purpose of an information attack at this level is to create false perceptions of both the internal organisational position, and the external environment. Thus, the aim is to create policies and strategies that are inappropriate for the organisation. The ultimate aim is the organisation's demise.

As well as falsifying or depriving information, emergency signals sent during urgent events can be withheld or delayed. Also, they can be made to occur erroneously (or very frequently) so they will be ignored in the future. S4 could also be 'flooded' with or fed erroneous information so causing confusion and mistrust of its validity.

The main task of an intelligence system's (S4) is to collect, process, analyse and produce, and disseminate information[4]. Therefore, the task of the attacker is to disrupt, deny, or manipulate data to provide the target with no information, or misinformation. If the target obtains data then the attacker's function is to provide misinformation to manipulate the context. For example, to imply that the data is incorrect (or, in fact, to imply incorrect information is correct). At the knowledge level, the attacker could provide further misinformation to interfere with the deductive and inductive processes needed to understand any information produced.

Notes

1 See Beer, S. (1984) The Viable System Model: its provenance, development, methodology and pathology, in: Espejo, R., Harnden, R. (eds) *The Viable System Model*, John Wiley & Sons, Chichester, pp. 211–270, and Beer, S. (1985). *Diagnosing the System for Organisations*. Wiley, Chichester.

2 See Espejo, R. (1993) Domains of interaction between a social system and its environment, *Systems Practice*, **6**, 5, p. 522.

3 From: Dearth, D.H., Williamson, C.A. (1996) Information Age/Information War, in: Campen, A.D., Dearth, D.H., Thomas Goodden, R. (eds) *Cyberwar: Security, Strategy, and Conflict in the Information Age*, AFCEA International Press, Fairfax, p. 25.

4 See Richelson, J.T. (1995) *The U.S. Intelligence Community –* third edition, Westview Press, Boulder, p. 3.

Appendix 3 | Checklist for deception

The concepts introduced in chapters 1 and 3 can provide a framework for developing a successful deception. Below are a number of questions to aid in formulating strategies and tactics.

What is the aim of the deception, and the desired end result?

Foremost in any planning for a deception must be the reason for carrying it out. Most deceptions are complicated affairs and rely on a series of interwoven strategies to provide the desired effect. For instance, altering a target database (that is, adding data either directly by changing their database, or indirectly by making only certain data available), and also working on the context of the situation by manipulating certain events, might be used to create an illusory effect.

An assessment of the likelihood of success needs to be made, and contingency plans drawn up. The plans are just that, and any situation is dynamic. Thus, contingencies are essential, as is constant monitoring of your efforts.

How are you going to measure the effect produced?

Using the desired end result as a benchmark, the actual effect produced needs to be assessed. How will you do this?

How will the attack be achieved?
The set of methods to be used needs to be established by

examining both the goals of the exercise and the feasibility of each method in this situation. Which one is the cheapest, most effective, and least risky?

What follow up measures need to occur?

If the campaign is successful, what follow-up measures are needed? Has the campaign opened up new opportunities? If it has been unsuccessful, what remedial measures need to be taken?

Table A3.1 gives the framework for attack planning in tabular form. The three main items are:

♦ **Elements of the target's system**: this lists the main parts of an information system as developed in chapter 1. Part of the strategy should be to pick the parts of the system most likely to be vulnerable and to achieve the desired result.

♦ **Method of deception**: this outlines the basic methods of deception. What is to be targeted: the data or knowledge?

♦ **Desired end result**: for each individual part of the attack the desired result should be determined, as should its relationship to other elements of the deception.

The other elements incorporated into any document with this table should be:

♦ **Overall aim of the deception.**

♦ **Overall desired end result.**

♦ **Legal implications.**

♦ **Possible negative effects and contingencies.**

♦ **People's roles and responsibilities.**

♦ **How are each of the methods used going to be integrated and co-ordinated?**

Table A3.1: Table for planning an information attack

ELEMENT OF TARGET'S SYSTEM		METHODS OF DECEPTION						DESIRED EFFECT
		Mask	Repackage	Dazzle	Mimic	Invent	Decoy	
SENSOR	Active							
	Passive							
OBJECT/EVENT								
PROCESSORS								
CONTAINERS								
RECORDERS								
CONTEXT								
HUMAN RECEIVER								
NETWORKS								

Appendix 4 | Retaliation against information attack: attitudes and practices of information systems managers

A4.1 Introduction

The problem of 'hackers' (or more correctly 'crackers') who damage, manipulate, steal, or destroy information is increasing. Schwartau[1] outlines the frustration of some American corporate managers with this phenomenon, and lists the following as the main causes of this:

♦ Hacking events are increasing by huge numbers.

♦ The assaults are becoming more aggressive and hostile.

♦ The attack tools are automated and require little technical skills.

♦ Political and social motivations have invited civil disobedience.

♦ Investigation of hacking events is very difficult.

♦ Law enforcement is not up to the task of investigating cyber crimes for lack of manpower, resources, and interest.

♦ Corporate America distrusts law enforcement to prosecute and keep any investigations secret.

The list below highlights a small variety of the activities that hackers have been known to engage in:

♦ Modification of medical records.

♦ Breach of military systems[2].

♦ Monitoring and alteration of telecommunications[3].

In many cases there have been reported incidents of hackers not only gaining unauthorised access (potentially breaching confidentiality), but also altering data or service provision (affecting integrity and/or availability).

As can be seen, breaches in all of the above categories of system offer significant opportunities to inflict damage (to both organisations and individuals) and, therefore, illustrate the nature of the hacker threat. Incidents such as those referenced indicate that many of our systems are vulnerable and that if someone has the inclination, and is willing to put in the effort, then existing security can often be breached. Furthermore, the evidence suggests that it is possible to breach systems that we would instinctively expect to be more secure (for example, military sites). The fact that such attacks are successful leaves systems vulnerable to more insidious threats than straightforward hacking, in which information systems become the target in a more sinister way.

Schwartau[4] postulates that because of the problem of hackers managers might take the law into their own hands, and retaliate causing damage to the attackers' equipment, software, and data. This is the concept of *cyber vigilantism*. In short, it is hacking the hackers. The military and intelligence services have developed much of the technology for this.

Organisational threats come not only from individuals but organised criminal and terrorist groups. Rathmell *et al.*[5]

posit the three main reasons for terrorist groups to use information warfare as raising funds, propaganda campaigns (mostly through web sites), and to attack the organisation's information infrastructure. It is these increasing threats for which organisations must prepare.

During the latter part of 1998, Winn Schwartau carried out an informal survey on the World Wide Web to establish a general impression of the attitudes of professionals in business and government to the concept of cyber vigilantism. The research presented in this appendix uses the basic idea of his survey to specifically seek out the attitudes of Australian IT managers to this 'offensive' attitude toward information security. Thus the results reflect the local Australian attitudes and these may not be assumed to reflect those present in other states. However, the results are interesting. No claim is made about the academic rigour of the survey. It was a 'quick and dirty' attempt to gauge the attitudes of IT managers toward this sensitive topic.

A4.2. Cyber vigilantism, the law, and ethics

Grace and Cohen[6] illustrate the dilemma in business of behaving ethically. They argue that all too often arguments are polarised into two choices:

♦ behave unethically, or

♦ fail.

For many organisations, business is a form of competitive warfare. Hence, techniques applicable to the military and intelligence services are viewed as feasible choices, although Grace and Cohen assert that it is wrong to assume that competitor's tactics are designed to destroy rivals. However, they do argue for an 'international legal and normative infrastructure. The point often lost in analogies with war, however, is that a great deal of this infrastructure already exists in private and public international law'[7]. Whilst this may be the case for general business practices, the advent of cyber-space has created problems of definition and jurisdiction.

Brenner[8], in her Model State Computer Crimes Codes, has attempted the specifics of defining cyber-vigilantism in legal terms. This is a conceptual legal model but has been used by some governments struggling with defining computer crimes. In section 8.08 of this code, the following is stated:

(a) *A person commits the offence of Cyber-vigilantism if he:*

    (1) *purposely or knowingly uses a computer, computer system, computer network, the Internet or any other online communication system;*

    (2) *acts without proper authorization or jurisdiction or exceeds the limits of his authorization or jurisdiction;*

    (3) *investigates or pursues alleged criminal activity or persons; and*

    (4) *commits an unlawful act*

(b) *A person who commits the offense of Cyber-vigilantism under Subsection (A) of this Section shall be guilty of any substantive crimes that are committed.*

(c) *It is not a defense to any substantive crimes committed that the person alleged to have engaged in Cyber-vigilantism was pursuing or investigating what he reasonably believed to be the commission of an illegal activity or the prior activities of an alleged criminal.*

It is interesting that paragraph (c) explicitly outlaws retaliation against illegal attacks.

However, over the last few years, legislation in America,

Europe, and Australia has allowed intelligence and law enforcement agencies to perform these operations. For instance in 1999, the Australia Security and Intelligence Organisation (ASIO) was allowed (with ministerial approval) to access data and generally 'hack' into systems. Therefore, legal hacking is the province of the authorities.

A4.3 Methodology used

The survey was sent out to 528 IT managers in two states of Australia (Western Australia and Victoria). This latter figure does not include 38 surveys which were returned because of incorrect addressing. The responses were anonymous. Each survey form was supplied with a prepaid envelope, and names of individuals or organisations were not required. As some of the questions were of a sensitive nature, this anonymity was thought to add to the validity of the data. The survey was sent out in February and March 1999. There were 111 valid responses, giving a response rate of 21% (61 from Western Australia and 50 from Victoria). Information on type of organisation is shown in table A4.1, and the size (determined by employee numbers) in table A4.2.

Table A4.1: Responses by organisational type

Organisational type	Responses	Percentage
Finance	11	10
Manufacturing	10	9
Mining	5	5
Wholesale	7	6
Retail	5	5
Government	28	25
Education	12	11
Other	33	29
Totals	111	100

Table A4.2: Responses by organisation size (respondents were asked to pick the largest size option that was applicable to them)

Organisation size	Responses	Percentage
<10	13	12
>10	5	5
>20	6	5
>50	10	9
>100	16	14
>250	14	13
>500	8	7
>1000	18	16
>5000	13	12
>10 000	8	7
Totals	111	100

A4.4 Rationale for each question

Table A4.3 lists the questions and the results for each. Each question had space for more specific comments. Also, there was an area for overall comments at the end of the questionnaire. Each of the questions was designed to discover either an attitude toward aggressive responses to information attack, or to find the level of organisational awareness for a particular aspect. The questions mentioned in this section can be found in table A4.3.

Question 1 'sets the scene' and partially establishes the respondent's attitude. Questions 3, 4, and 5 develop this by establishing the attitude toward their own situation (question 3), the level of attack it is appropriate to respond to (questions 4a–4e), and to see if there was any contradiction (question 5, which asks if it is more appropriate for the 'authorities' to respond rather than themselves).

Question 2 ascertains the respondent's knowledge of previous attacks.

Question 8 establishes if any policies have been established in relation to hacker attacks. It was assumed that those organisations, which had been attacked were more likely to have policies for these events.

Question 6 was designed to establish the respondent's attitude toward the right of an organisation's system to exist. It is coupled with question 7, which establishes the attitude toward their own system's 'rights'.

Question 10 has the dual purpose of establishing the level of perceived threat from competitors, and consequently, the perceived level of competitors' ethics, their own level of security, and perhaps the effectiveness of the judicial system.

A4.5 Results and discussion

Attitude toward aggressive response

Table A4.3 contains the basic answers given in the survey. The first question established that a significant majority of respondents (73%) agreed, in principle, with someone else (the Pentagon) 'striking back' to an attack. There was no pattern in the written comments to this question. Comments ranged from concern about legality, for example:

♦ 'Seems appropriate but is it legal?'

to a satisfaction that something is being done:

♦ 'One for the good guys.'

When asked about their **own** responses to an attack (question 3), the respondents seemed less sure. Although a

Table A4.3: Survey questions and percentage responses

Question	Answers (% of total)		
	Yes	No	?
1. Recently, the Pentagon responded to a series of hacker attacks by striking back with software, which disabled the attackers' browsers. Do you think this was a valid and appropriate response?	73	23	4
2. To your knowledge has your organisation ever been the victim of an attack?	14	80	6
3. Do you feel that your organisation has a right to respond to an attack in this manner?	65	30	5
4. When do you think it is valid to respond to an attack?			
a. Someone attempts to enter your network?	70	24	6
b. Someone reads some of your system data?	80	16	4
c. Someone reads some of your applications data?	81	16	4
d. Someone attempts to alter data?	90	9	1
e. Someone tries to destroy a part of your system?	93	6	1
5. Is it more appropriate to allow the authorities and the legal system to deal with hackers?	60	26	14
6. Do people have the right to attack child pornography and other 'controversial' web sites?	23	64	13
7. Do you feel that your organisation has the right to expect others to respect the integrity of your sites?	98	0	2
8. Has your organisation developed a policy about dealing with such things as hacker attacks?	33	60	7
9. Has your organisation investigated offensive software?	20	73	7
10. Do you believe an attack from a competitor organisation is a real threat?	30	66	4

majority (65%) agreed it was appropriate to respond, it was less than that for others to retaliate. This may have been a reflection of the example (the Pentagon) where some respondents perceived 'national security' as being an overriding element. The majority of comments expressed concern about the legality of the action, for example:

♦ 'I would have to seek legal advice before I attack back.'

♦ 'May be a problem legally.'

♦ 'Must stay within the legal system.'

Others reinforced the need for some sort of response:

♦ 'Certainly there needs to be a response level.'

♦ 'History has shown that being passive is only an invite to do it again.'

By and large, the comments showed support for striking back over and above other considerations:

♦ 'Two wrongs do not make it right versus protection of my space and property. The latter wins.'

Question 4 investigates the trigger point for retaliation. The question presents events of increasing damage to a system. As the potential damage increases, the support rises from 70% to 93%. There seems a slight contradiction in these answers. Although only 65% of respondents supported actively responding to an attack in question 3, 70% support a response for an attempt to enter a network in question 4. Strangely, the comments are also much more aggressive and assertive in tone, for example:

♦ 'Any attack should not be tolerated.'

♦ 'Entry without prior advice or authority equals trespass.'

However, despite the overwhelming (93%) agreement to

response to an attempt to destroy a part of the system, there still appears to be trepidation present:

♦ 'Yes, but only after a warning has been given, otherwise it may be an innocent browser.'

♦ 'How do you distinguish an attack from something else?'

♦ 'Respond in the sense of stopping the attack, not striking back.'

Contradiction in the responses is also exposed in the answers to question 5, which deals with the appropriateness of the 'authorities' to deal with hackers. Schwartau contends that frustration with the legal process and other official channels has a large influence on American management's support of strike back options. However, the respondents to this survey showed support for preferentially using the authorities to solve the problem (60%). This seems to conflict with the answers to questions 3 and 4, where there is majority support for organisational response. It is perhaps reflective of the desired state of affairs rather than the practical aspects of the situation. For instance, question 3 asks for support in principle of striking back, and, although it did get majority support, this was not as high as when the specifics of question 4 were outlined. The comments for question 5 also expose some interesting views, for example:

♦ 'Needs a dual approach.'

♦ 'Both needed. Authorities determine their own priorities based on dollar value of damage done. Not appropriate.'

♦ 'What authority? What time frame? What stops the hacker in the meantime?'

Expanding on this last comment, many of the others also reflect on the time element of official response, for example:

♦ 'Ineffective and too slow – how can they react in time?'

♦ 'Too slow and uncertain.'

Other comments expose the enormity of effective official response, for example:

♦ 'Are you kidding? Across international borders and with no ability to establish definite proof.'

♦ 'They may have no way of tracing the offender after the event.'

♦ 'They won't get their act together in time.'

However, the contradictions may not be as wide as stated. Only 34 respondents answered 'yes' to both questions 3 and 5. Of these, 47% who thought it right to respond themselves, also thought it more appropriate that the authorities do so (54% of those who thought it appropriate for the authorities also thought it was all right for themselves to retaliate). From this, it can be established that about one half had the conflicting opinion that they should retaliate themselves and it was more appropriate for the authorities to do so.

Organisational awareness, threats, and response

It appears from question 2 that the majority of respondents (80%) have not experienced (or have knowledge of) an attack on their systems. This probably reflects effective security. Paradoxically, it can also expose a weak monitoring system. Whatever the reasons, it gives no real incentive to research or produce policies and procedures to deal with attacks, except at the general risk management process within the organisation. This is reflected in the answers to question 8, where 60% of the respondents declare they have no policy for dealing with hackers. Only 53% (8 out of 15) of those who had recognised that they had been attacked had a policy. Strangely, only 22% of those who had a policy (8 out of 36) said they had been attacked. Most comments to question 8 declare 'passive' security measures, for example:

♦ 'We have firewalls, etc. Preventive rather than attack.'

♦ 'In a sense, as we have installed firewalls, system security, and access control.'

The lack of attacks also accounts for the majority of respondents not investigating 'offensive software'. Many of the respondents confused the context of the word 'offensive', assuming it to mean such things as pornography, or viruses. If there is no perceived need for a product why investigate it, or even know what it means?

The threat of an organised attack from a competitor (question 10) does not appear to be a concern for the majority of respondents (66%). Some do not even recognise that they have competitors, for example:

♦ 'Government agency. No competitors.'

♦ 'Charity providing services to clients.'

♦ 'No, not in our business.'

These responses may be derived from a narrow view of what a competitor is, but do imply a lack of thought about potential aggressors. For example, comments such as:

♦ 'Perhaps, but not yet possible.'

♦ 'Not competitors, but malicious individuals.'

Indicate that the threat is not thought to be great. A number of respondents did comment that the idea of using system attacks as a competitive tool was a novel one, for example:

♦ 'Had not thought of that angle. Interesting thought.'

Of those that had registered an attack (that is, saying 'yes' to question 2), 53% (8 out of 15) did not think that they had anything to fear in this area from their competitors. Of those who did not recognise a threat from their competitors (73), only 11% had registered an attack.

The impression given is that, at this moment in time, ethical business practice and/or the legal system will stop competitors from these aggressive acts. Of course, it could be lack of exposure to the techniques which has caused little consideration of the possibilities.

System integrity

Not surprisingly, 98% of the respondents thought that others should respect the integrity of their own site (question 7). The main thrust of the comments was that their 'property rights' were sacrosanct, for example:

♦ 'It is property the same as physical property.'

♦ 'Most definite on this.'

♦ 'Yes, as I have the right to expect for any of my property.'

There was no confusion in these replies. However, the responses to question 6 revealed some contradictions.

Whilst 64% of respondents did feel that controversial sites should have their integrity respected, 23% said it was a right to attack them (13% did not know). Of those who did think it right to attack controversial sites (25), 96% insisted on the integrity of their own sites. Only 22% of those who expected their site to be respected also thought it right to attack a contentious site. Whilst most comments expressed the opinion that the authorities should deal with this type of site. For example:

♦ 'The law should stop these sites.'

♦ 'The law should cover these issues.'

There seems to be a dilemma here. Many comments expressed the view that internet sites should be free to all opinions, and that without this, the system would be compromised. For example:

♦ 'Must protect freedom of speech. This is up to authorities not individuals.'

♦ 'What is controversial? Who is the umpire that can ensure political, racial, religious, etc. overtones are not used to stop web sites?'

♦ 'No, but I understand how they feel.'

However, the contrast between the answers to questions 6 and 7 does show potential dilemmas, and inherent self-justification for attacking certain sites.

General comments

The general comments from respondents illustrate other issues. Some respondents put the onus on the victim, for example:

♦ 'Organisations with poor security have no right to use retaliation as a deterrent. This is no different to booby-trapping your car in case someone steals it …'

♦ 'Hacking is an invasion of one's private business and needs to be harshly treated by the law. It is up to us to protect ourselves, but not to take the law into our own hands.'

Others reflect that hacking is wrong no matter who does it:

♦ 'I believe that there needs to be a complete understanding that hacking is not a justifiable course of action for anyone to take.'

♦ 'If a burglar breaks into my house, can I attack him? Could I attack his house in a similar way? Probably not ...'

Another response puts an interesting slant on semantics:

'The word attack is an emotive word. If access was simply the question, the answer may be different.'

Notes

[1] See Schwartau, W. (1999) *Corporate Vigilantism Survey Results*. (12/1/99).
URL: http://www.infowar.com

[2] See Niccolai, J. (1998) Israeli Arrested for Hacking U.S. Military Computers, *IDG News* Service, March 19, 1998.

[3] See Littman, J. (1997) *The Watchman – The Twisted Life and Crimes of Serial Hacker Kevin Poulsen*, Little & Brown Company Limited, USA.

[4] Schwartau, W. (1999) *Corporate Vigilantism Survey Results*. (12/1/99).
URL:http://www.infowar.com

[5] Rathmell, A., Overill, R., Valeri, L. and Gearson, J. (1997) 'The IW Threat from Sub-State Groups: an Interdisciplinary Approach, presented at *Third International Symposium on Command and Control Research and Technology*, 17–20 June 1997.
URL: http://www.kcl.ac.uk/orgs/icsa

[6] Grace, D., Cohen, S. (1998) *Business Ethics* – second edition, Oxford University Press, Melbourne.

[7] Ibid, p. 181.

[8] Brenner, S. (1998) *Model State Computer Crimes Code*.
URL http://www.cybercrimes.net/MSCCC/MSCCCMain.html# Article 8 (accessed 5 May 1999).

Discussion questions

Introduction

1. Is the concept of 'war' useful in the contemporary business world when formulating competitive strategies?

2. Is it the responsibility of the information systems/services manager to facilitate the aggressive use of the corporate database? If not, who is responsible?

3. Is information a critical factor in an organisation's survival? If so, why is it?

4. Is 'information superiority' important in the market place?

Chapter 1

1. Do you agree with the model presented in chapter 1 of the relationships between data, information, and knowledge? Can you think of any others? What are the limitations of the model offered?

2. What legal and ethical issues do you think are raised by information warfare? Relate your discussion to the idea of attacking data and knowledge as presented in this chapter?

3. How can you change the context of a situation or people's perception of it?

4. In terms of the model presented in figure 1.3, design attack strategies for each element for an organisational circumstance you are familiar with. Outline the implications for both your organisation and the target. Include the objectives of each strategy.

5. Why is speed of response to an attack so important in today's world?

6. Can you stop a 'surprise' attack?

7. Has the development of the 'networked society' made economically advanced communities more or less vulnerable?

Chapter 2

1. Does your organisation possess a specific intelligence function? If so, what are its responsibilities?

2. Is counter-intelligence a useful concept in today's corporate world?

3. What benefits are there in corporate espionage? What valuable vulnerable information assets does your organisation possess? Discuss in terms of operational, tactical, and strategic information.

4. What environmental data does your organisation collect? Is the collection timely and is the data disseminated effectively? What data is not collected that should be?

5. Does data have value? If it does, grade the data in your corporate database in terms of value to your organisation.

6. How does your organisation cope with detrimental information presented to clients, government agencies, the media, or the public?

7. Is it good business practice to actively produce negative information about competitors, or other corporate 'enemies' such as pressure groups? Is it ethical? Does that matter?

Chapter 3

1. Deception is often described in negative terms by 'equivalent' words such as: sham, con, pretext, cheat, trickery, lie, delude, betray, swindle, hoodwink, defraud, dupe, and mislead. Many of these words imply a motive as well as an action. Describe situations where deception can be a positive activity? Is motive important?

2. Using the six types of deception described in section 3.2, develop a tactic for each, relevant to your situation.

3. What criteria do you use to assess whether data is authentic?

4. Can you rely on anything being 'real' in the digital world?

5. How does your organisation determine what data is authentic and what is not? Is mission critical data handled any differently from the unimportant? Are sources of data ever verified? How?

6. Does anyone check output (for example, the corporate web page) for impact?

7. Is your corporate web page checked for integrity on a regular basis?

8. Does your organisation 'lie'? If so, when and why?

9. What are the positive and negative implications of the 'surveillance society'? Is it a threat to individual freedom?

10. Can any electronically produced and stored data be trusted totally? What are the characteristics needed for a trusted system?

Chapter 4

1. How could your organisation be attacked?

2. Has your organisation taken steps to reduce the risks of being attacked?

3. Has your organisation plans in place to deal with an attack?

Chapter 5

1. Does your organisation have the right to attack on-line attackers?

2. Does your organisation have the tools to carry out such attacks?

3. Do you know the legal ramifications within your country if you are caught retaliating to your on-line attackers?

Chapter 6

1. Has your organisation a real time method of detecting attacks?

2. What would be the impact of a denial-of-service attack upon your organisation?

3. What plans does your organisation have to protect itself against a denial-of-service attack?

Chapter 7

1. For your organisation, list the impacts (both internal and external) of the types of attacks mentioned in the IWRAM model.

Chapter 8

1. Does your organisation's upper management really value the corporate data, and its potential?

2. Does the knowledge/information systems manager have the appropriate authority to develop strategies to fully utilise the data and knowledge in your organisation?

3. What are the hindrances for converting the computer services function to a truly information system function?

Chapter 9

1. What institution(s) should develop laws for I-War? Could they ever be enforced or effective?

2. What laws could your organisation use to defend itself?

Chapter 10

1. Should terrorist groups be allowed to use web sites?

2. If 'extremist' groups were banned from using the Web, who could enforce the regulation, would it be effective, and what are the dangers of such an action?

Chapter 11

1. What do you think will be the most popular technologically based extensions of human senses? What are the dangers of these?

2. Do you think perceptually based output can override 'common sense'?

3. Describe some applications for wearable computers and how they can be abused.

Chapter 12

1. In the future, will any confidential data be safely transmitted electronically? What are the alternatives?

2. Speculate about possible future technologies and their implications for I-War.

Useful web sites

www.infowar.com

This is a very useful site for all I-War information. It has a daily update of interesting events worldwide. There are numerous useful links. This is must to view if you are interested in I-War and want to keep up to date. The site sponsors the annual InfoWarCon conferences in Washington and London.

www.iwar.org

This is the site for the Centre for Infra-structural Warfare Studies. It has been renamed RMA (Revolution in Military Affairs) Watch. The name gives the emphasis of the site, but some useful intelligence reports can be found there. Not very active in 2000.

www.kcl.ac.uk/orgs/icsa

This is the site for the International Centre for Security Analysis at King's College London. The I-War section was stagnant in 1999 but seems to have come back to life in 2000. It has some useful links and some interesting downloadable papers.

www.rand.org

This is the site of the Rand Institute in the USA. It provides policy reports for the US government. Some of the reports are downloadable. There is a group in RAND who are interested in information and netwar. Some of their reports are influential, so it is worth visiting this site now and again.

www.terrorism.com/infowar

This is the site of the Terrorism Research Institute. It has recently become reactivated in 2000. There is much up-to-date information, downloadable papers, etc. Worth regular visits.

www.dodccrp.org

This site is sponsored by the US Department of Defense. It has numerous downloadable and free books in the area of I-War. It has a military bias, but many of the documents also cover economic warfare aspects. The books can also be obtained free of charge if you do not want to download them.

Glossary of terms

Counter-intelligence

This describes the functions of protecting your own information, as well as attempting to disrupt the information processes of an 'enemy'.

Cracker

This is used to describe a malicious hacker.

Cyber terrorism

This covers terrorist activities based on the use and abuse of computer networks to further their cause. Usually associated with damage done to systems.

Cyber vigilantism

The act of retaliating against a computer attack by attacking the offending computer system.

Cyberwar

This is a term not used in this book, but is often meant to mean aggressive actions on computer networks. It tends to be associated with military situations but is also used with abandon in other fields.

Data

Data describes attributes of physical and abstract 'things'. Hence an address is an attribute of an individual, or upper speed is an attribute of a car. It is the raw material needed to produce information, and is what is stored on computer systems.

Data is technically a plural word (singular 'datum'). However, it has become common to use it as a singular word (as in this book) to describe a set of attributes.

Denial-of-service

Usually used to describe an attack on an ISP or other computer systems which results in the users being unable to access the services of that system.

Hacker

This describes a person who attempts to penetrate another computer system without permission. Hackers are usually seen not to be malicious, unlike crackers.

HTML

This is an acronym for Hypertext Markup Language. This language allows a file to be created, which can be displayed as a Web page and have hypertext links.

Information

The subset of extracted from the data available by people (or some intelligent machine) using the knowledge available to them and also the context of the problem.

Information warfare (I-War)

This describes the full extent of the use of information for aggressive purposes. It can refer to activities from the physical destruction of IT equipment to the use of information in subtle ways to influence decision makers.

Intelligence

This describes both a product and a process. The process is the planning for, acquisition and analysis of, data. The product of this process is also called intelligence (that is, analysed data). It is similar to the way the term 'information' is used in this text.

Intrusion

An illegal entry into your system.

Intrusion Detection System (IDS)

A software system that detects intrusions.

IP (Internet Protocol)

A part of the TCP/IP protocol which ensures that messages get to the correct destination. An **IP address** identifies a host on a TCP/IP area wide network.

ISP

An abbreviation for an Internet Service Provider.

Knowledge

The set of interpreted data and mental skills possessed by individuals which has been influenced by education, biology, socialisation, experience, culture, and many other factors affecting the individual involved.

Network

A collection of nodes connected in someway. A network is often used to mean a collection of computer-based equipment connected by telecommunications. However, it can also mean a collection of almost anything as long as they have real or abstract connections to each other.

Netwar

A term similar to 'cyberwar' except this is usually meant to refer to social rather than military conflict. It is not used in this text.

Perceptual intelligence

This is the ability to deal with the current situation. You can perceive variables which are pertinent to the situation and react to it. Humans have this facility. However, developments with hardware/software are producing inanimate items which are capable of a form of perceptual intelligence as well (see chapter 11).

Spoofing

The act of pretending to be another identity. Hence, an attacker will take on a false address identity when attacking another system, therefore, tracking back will reveal an identity other than the attacker's.

TCP (Transmission Control Protocol)

This part of the TCP/IP protocol breaks down and reassembles messages into packets.

Bibliography

Listed below are some further useful texts about I-War:

Adams, J. (1998) *The Next World War*, Hutchinson, London.

Alberts, D.S., Garstka, J.J. and Stein, F.P. (1999) *Network Centric Warfare: Developing and Leveraging Information Superiority* – second edition, CCRP Publications, Vienna, VA.

Arquilla, J., Ronfeldt, D., (eds) (1997) *In Athena's Camp: Preparing for Conflict in the Information Age*, Rand Corporation, Santa Monica.

Arquilla, J., Ronfeldt, D. (1996) *The Advent of Netwar*, Rand Corporation, Santa Monica.

Campen, A.D., Dearth, D.H. (eds) (1998) *Cyberwar 2.0: Myths, Mysteries and Reality*, AFCEA International Press, Fairfax.

Campen, A.D., Dearth, D.H. and Thomas Goodden, R. (eds) (1996) *Cyberwar: Security, Strategy, and Conflict in the Information Age*, AFCEA International Press, Fairfax.

Denning, D.E. (1999) *Information Warfare and Security*, Addison Wesley, Reading, Mass.

Forno, R., Baklarz, R. (1999) *The Art of Information Warfare* – second edition, Universal Publishers.

Gauntlett, A. (1999) *Net Spies*, Vision Paperbacks, London.

Nichols, R.K., Ryan, D.J. and Ryan, J.J.C.H. (2000) *Defending Your Digital Assets*, McGraw-Hill, New York.

Schwartau, W. (2000) *Cybershock,* Thunder's Mouth Press, New York.

Schwartau, W. (1996) *Information Warfare* – second edition, Thunder's Mouth Press, New York.

Toffler, A., Toffler, H. (1993) *War and Anti-War*, Warren Books, London.

Waltz, E. (1998) *Information Warfare – Principles and Operations*. Artech House, Norwood.

Winkler, I. (1997) *Corporate Espionage*, Prima Publishing, USA.

Index

For Product Safety Concerns and Information please contact our EU
representative GPSR@taylorandfrancis.com Taylor & Francis Verlag GmbH,
Kaufingerstraße 24, 80331 München, Germany

Printed and bound by CPI Group (UK) Ltd, Croydon, CR0 4YY

08/05/2025

01864489-0004